THE ASSERTIVE TRAINER

Latest titles in the McGraw-Hill Training Series

LEARNING THROUGH SIMULATIONS
A Guide to the Design and Use of Simulations in Business and Education
John Fripp   ISBN 0-07-707588-9
MEETINGS MANAGEMENT
A Manual of Effective Training Material
Leslie Rae   ISBN 0-07-707782-2
WORKSHOPS THAT WORK
100 Ideas to Make Your Training Events More Effective
Tom Bourner, Vivien Martin,
Phil Race   ISBN 0-07-707800-4
TRAINING FOR PROFIT
A Guide to the Integration of Training in an Organization's Success
Philip Darling   ISBN 0-07-707786-5
THE HANDBOOK FOR ORGANIZATIONAL CHANGE
Strategy and Skill for Trainers and Developers
Carol A. O'Connor   ISBN 0-07-707693-1
MANAGING THE TRAINING PROCESS
Mike Wills   ISBN 0-07-707806-3
DEVELOPING DIRECTORS
Building An Effective Boardroom Team
Colin Coulson-Thomas   ISBN 0-07-707590-0
RESOURCE-BASED LEARNING
Using Open and Flexible Resources for Continuous Development
Julie Dorrell   ISBN 0-07-707692-3
FACILITATION
Providing Opportunities For Learning
Trevor Bentley   ISBN 0-07-707684-2
DEVELOPMENT CENTRES
Realizing the Potential of Your Employees Through Assessment and
Development
Geoff Lee and
David Beard   ISBN 0-07-707785-7
DEVELOPING MANAGERS AS COACHES
A Trainer's Guide
Frank Salisbury   ISBN 0-07-707892-6
TEAM BUILDING
A Practical Guide for Trainers
Neil Clark   ISBN 0-07-707846-2
PRACTICAL INSTRUCTIONAL DESIGN FOR OPEN LEARNING
MATERIALS
A Modular Course Covering Open Learning, Computer Based Training,
Multimedia
Nigel Harrison   ISBN 0-07-709055-1

Details of these and other titles in the series are available from:
The Product Manager, Professional Books, McGraw-Hill Book Company Europe,
Shoppenhangers Road, Maidenhead, Berkshire SL6 2QL
Tel: 0628 23432 Fax: 0628 770224

The assertive trainer

A practical handbook on assertiveness for trainers
and running assertiveness courses

Liz Willis and Jenny Daisley

McGRAW-HILL BOOK COMPANY

London · New York · St Louis · San Francisco · Auckland
Bogotá · Caracas · Lisbon · Madrid · Mexico · Milan
Montreal · New Delhi · Panama · Paris · San Juan · São Paulo
Singapore · Sydney · Tokyo · Toronto

Published by
McGRAW-HILL Book Company Europe
Shoppenhangers Road, Maidenhead, Berkshire, SL6 2QL, England
Telephone 01628 23432
Fax 01628 770224

British Library Cataloguing in Publication Data
Willis, Liz
    Assertive Trainer: Practical Handbook on
Assertiveness for Trainers and Running
Assertiveness Courses. – (McGraw-Hill
Training Series)
I. Title   II. Daisley, Jenny   III. Series
658.31244

    ISBN 0-07-709077-2

Library of Congress Cataloging-in-Publication Data
The CIP data of this title is available from the Library of Congress,
Washington DC, USA

12345 CL 98765

Typeset by BookEns Limited, Baldock, Herts.
and printed and bound in Great Britain by Clays Ltd., St Ives plc.

Contents

Series preface

Training and development are now firmly centre stage in most organizations, if not all. Nothing unusual in that—for some organizations. They have always seen training and development as part of the heart of their businesses—but more and more must see it that same way.

The demographic trends through the 1990s will inject into the marketplace severe competition for good people who will need good training. Young people without conventional qualifications, skilled workers in redundant crafts, people out of work, women wishing to return to work—all will require excellent training to fit them to meet the job demands of the 1990s and beyond.

But excellent training does not spring from what we have done well in the past. T&D specialists are in a new ball game. 'Maintenance' training— training to keep up skill levels to do what we have always done—will be less in demand. Rather, organization, work and market change training are now much more important and will remain so for some time. Changing organizations and people is no easy task, requiring special skills and expertise which, sadly, many T&D specialists do not possess.

To work as a 'change' specialist requires us to get to centre stage—to the heart of the company's business. This means we have to ask about future goals and strategies, and even be involved in their development, at least as far as T&D policies are concerned.

This demands excellent communication skills, political expertise, negotiating ability, diagnostic skills—indeed, all the skills a good internal consultant requires.

The implications for T&D specialists are considerable. It is not enough merely to be skilled in the basics of training, we must also begin to act like business people and to think in business terms and talk the language of business. We must be able to resource training not just from within but by using the vast array of external resources. We must be able to manage our activities as well as any other manager. We must share in the creation and communication of the company's vision. We must never let the goals of the company out of our sight.

In short, we may have to grow and change with the business. It will be hard. We shall have to demonstrate not only relevance but also value for money and achievement of results. We shall be our own boss, as accountable for results as any other line manager, and we shall have to deal with fewer internal resources.

The challenge is on, as many T&D specialists have demonstrated to me over the past few years. We need to be capable of meeting that challenge. This is why McGraw-Hill Book Company Europe have planned and launched this major new training series—to help us meet that challenge.

The series covers all aspects of T&D and provides the knowledge base from which we can develop plans to meet the challenge. They are practical books for the professional person. They are a starting point for planning our journey into the twenty-first century.

Use them well. Don't just read them. Highlight key ideas, thoughts, action pointers or whatever, and have a go at doing something with them. Through experimentation we evolve; through stagnation we die.

I know that all the authors in the McGraw-Hill Training Series would want me to wish you good luck. Have a great journey into the twenty-first century.

ROGER BENNETT
Series Editor

About the series editor

Roger Bennett has over 20 years' experience in training, management education, research and consulting. He has long been involved with trainer training and trainer effectiveness. He has carried out research into trainer effectiveness, and conducted workshops, seminars, and conferences on the subject around the world. He has written extensively on the subject including the book *Improving Trainer Effectiveness*, Gower. His work has taken him all over the world and has involved directors of companies as well as managers and trainers.

Dr Bennett has worked in engineering, several business schools (including the International Management Centre, where he launched the UK's first masters degree in T&D), and has been a board director of two companies. He is the editor of the *Journal of European Industrial Training* and was series editor of the ITD's *Get In There* workbook and video package for the managers of training departments. He now runs his own business called The Management Development Consultancy.

About the authors

Liz Willis and **Jenny Daisley** are consultants with over 37 years' combined experience in the training and development field who are well known as pioneers and innovators in the area of women's development training. They each run their own consultancies, The Springboard Consultancy and Biographic Management respectively, and collaborate on projects and on writing together.

Liz and Jenny work at all levels in organizations, developing overall strategies as well as designing and delivering a variety of training and development events from in-depth residential courses with small groups, to one day workshops with hundreds. They work nationally in the UK, in the private, public, and voluntary sectors and also internationally in Australia, New Zealand and Eastern and Western Europe.

Their consultancy work takes a positive and down-to-earth approach, which, together with their earlier careers as line managers in the private and public sectors, gives them the unusual blend of the practical manager with the experienced, creative developer.

They are most well known for the development and delivery of The Springboard Women's Development Programme, the three-month personal and work development programme for non-management women, which was recognized in 1991 with The Lady Platt Award and in 1993 with a National Training Award for outstanding quality and excellence in training. The programme currently runs in the UK, Australia, New Zealand, France and Denmark through a network of over 250 Springboard trainers who have been trained and accredited by Liz and Jenny.

Liz and Jenny prefer to work developmentally, building on strengths and finding, with their clients, solutions which are practical and flexible in today's changing world. Through this approach they found assertiveness to be especially useful and started running assertiveness training in the early 1980s both as stand-alone courses and incorporated into longer personal development and management development programmes.

In more recent years they have been heavily in demand for training trainer events. All their work with trainers, whether it is on design, delivery, evaluation or internal PR, always includes training trainers in assertiveness as they believe this to be one of the most effective and appropriate skills for trainers.

This is the third book they have written together.

Acknowledgements

We are very aware of the many and varied contributions to this book and of the support and help which we've received. It's a pleasure for us to thank everyone who has helped us:

- the hundreds of men and women who have worked with us as participants on our assertiveness courses who, consciously or unconsciously, have challenged our abilities to be assertive and therefore have expanded our experience and skills of assertiveness and provided us with many of the examples in the book
- the men and women who have worked with us as clients and co-trainers, who have shared with us the rewards and difficulties of introducing assertiveness into organizations and so have also contributed to this book.
- the many other assertiveness trainers and consultants who have contributed so much to an increasing acceptance of assertiveness, most notably Ken and Kate Back and Anne Dickson.
- Chris Fernie of the Equal Opportunities Commission for his help and advice on the legal position of single-gender training.
- Carroll Beard, once again, for her word processing skills and ability to understand our handwriting and constant changes, miraculously resulting in a readable manuscript at the end!

We are especially grateful to everyone who took the time and trouble to write the case studies which make the ideas in the book come to life, in particular the staff at BT who contributed three case studies:

- Carolann Ashton of BBC Network Television
- Christine Baines of Christine Baines Consultancy
- Jane Beck of Jane Beck Associates
- Jackie Campbell of The Woolwich Building Society
- Lorraine Chimes of Barking and Dagenham Council for Voluntary Service
- Janette Fiddaman of Littlewoods Home Shopping Division
- Pete Hodgson of BT
- Alison Hustwitt of Gloucester City Volunteer Bureau
- Mairi Macleod of Mairi Macleod Associates
- Barbara Peel of The Learning Curve
- Colin Russell of BT

Acknowledgements

- Deborah Smith of The Macro Group
- Nicky Stevenson of The Guild
- Simon Templar of BT
- Deborah Uí Dhaibhéid of Newry Volunteer Bureau
- Stella Wiseman

1 Setting the scene

This book is for all trainers and people involved in training, not just those who run courses in assertiveness. It includes freelance trainers and those working inside organizations; those who have never worked in any way with assertiveness and those who already run assertiveness courses. Whatever your current level of assertiveness, if you work as a trainer, train as part of your management responsibilities, or are about to begin work as a trainer, then this book is for you.

The book has two main themes: firstly, the relevance of assertiveness to trainers whilst running mainstream courses, and secondly, running courses in assertiveness. However, although it will give you ideas and material to use on assertiveness courses, it does not qualify you to run them. If, having read this book, you want to run your own assertiveness courses, nominate yourself for one of the training trainer courses described in the appendix.

In our combined 37 years' experience as trainers we have run developmental and skills courses for a wide variety of groups of people: women-only groups, men-only groups, mixed-gender groups, directors, senior, middle and junior management, clerical, secretarial, technical, manual staff, part-time staff, full-time staff, contract staff and freelance people. All these courses have had one thing in common: the aim has been to effect change in knowledge, skill or behaviour. When people are faced with having to change, they do not usually automatically accept it unquestioningly; they are often resistant or questioning of what is being suggested, so that they can understand it more fully. Additionally, they may be fearful of change for its own sake, or afraid that the process of change will make them lose face.

All trainers are, at some stage, challenged by participants on their courses, in terms of their own knowledge, ability, or past experience. They also need to be open to feedback about their own performance and personalities so that training becomes and remains as effective as possible. To set up training programmes and courses trainers may need to negotiate with, and have dealings with, people with whom they will not necessarily see eye to eye. From the germ of an idea for training and development through to the final evaluation and report, trainers are constantly tested, in terms of their ability to be open, straightforward, honest, able to move things on and reach satisfactory conclusions. So the whole process of being a trainer demands inter-personal skills of a high standard, constantly in use, and constantly under scrutiny.

When training trainers, and in continuing to work with trainers as associates and colleagues, we constantly find that the answer to many of the situations which arise, or which may potentially arise, for trainers lies in the use of assertiveness.

This book briefly recalls the history of assertiveness, looks at its current application, and gives the definition and ingredients of assertiveness. It examines how assertiveness applies in all stages of training, and in addition, gives hints and tips about specific courses on assertiveness, and looks in detail at the role of the assertive trainer in all these stages.

The book follows a logical progression from examining why organizations and individual trainers need assertiveness in training, through to setting up and running programmes and being assertive whilst delivering mainstream training courses. In the final chapters we look at running specific assertiveness courses and the role of assertiveness in the evaluation of any training. Chapter 6, on assertiveness courses, should not be read in isolation, as it builds on all the material in preceding chapters.

The objectives of this book are to enable trainers to:

- understand the usefulness and application of assertiveness in training generally
- assess their abilities to be assertive in a wide range of training situations
- develop their own assertiveness skills
- develop and run top-quality assertiveness training courses

Throughout the book, we have used the word 'trainer' to mean anyone engaged in any form of training: formal or informal, freelance, voluntary or employed. The word 'organization' is used to mean any form of organization, however large or small, commercial, public sector or voluntary. The word 'course' is used to mean the piece of training, which could also be a workshop, distance learning, work shadowing, open learning or on-the-job training. The word 'programme' is used to mean an overall programme of training which may consist of several courses and have a strategic objective inside the organization.

The history of assertiveness

The roots of assertiveness lie in the Civil Rights Movement in the USA in the 1960s, where it was recognized that people from ethnic minorities, and specifically black people, needed to find a way to cope with the aggression, oppression and discrimination that they faced. Fighting aggression with aggression did not always seem to reach any successful conclusions. Nor did placidly accepting the aggression, as, even when people behaved outwardly placidly, inwardly they were burning with anger and frustration. The original work on assertiveness was based substantially on techniques which could easily be learned and copied. These techniques were effective because they constituted a response radically different to that which people had normally experienced. They gave power to the people using them, and enabled them to feel a new self-respect as they stood up for themselves in a positive way.

In the late 1960s Transactional Analysis rose to popularity when Thomas Harris (1967) explained the four 'life positions' based on your feelings about yourself and others as:

- I'm not OK—you're OK
- I'm not OK—you're not OK
- I'm OK—you're not OK
- I'm OK—you're OK

Harris build on the work of Eric Berne (1964) about the games that people play in their relationships. Both established that we can change the behaviour that we have learned. Three of these four life positions describe behaviours related to assertiveness which are described in Chapter 2:

- I'm not OK—you're OK   = passivity
- I'm not OK—you're not OK = depression
- I'm OK—you're not OK   = aggression
- I'm OK—you're OK   = assertion

Transactional Analysis indicates that the first three life positions are unconscious, having evolved as a result of conditioning in earlier life, whilst the fourth life position involving assertiveness (I'm OK—you're OK) is the result of a conscious decision.

This concept of making a decision that 'we are both OK' underlies the subsequent theories of assertiveness which developed in the late 1960s.

The 1960s

Manual J. Smith, a clinical experimental psychologist working at the Peace Corps Training and Development Center in 1969, recognized that Peace Corps Trainees had little preparation for 'coping with every-day human interaction problems' (Smith, 1975). Similarly, in two therapeutic situations with people with behaviour problems, mild phobias and even severe neurotic disorders and schizophrenias, he found the same inadequacy as with the Peace Corps trainees: 'Many of the patients seemed incapable of coping with critical statements or questions about themselves from other people'.

Smith's experimental work on helping people to deal with criticism became the forerunner of assertiveness as it is known today. By 1975 the assertiveness therapy which he recorded in *When I Say No I Feel Guilty* had been clinically evaluated and systematically and successfully used by Smith and his colleagues.

The approach centred around a 'bill of rights', reproduced here from Smith (1975):

A bill of assertive rights

- You have the right to judge your own behaviour, thoughts, and emotions, and to take the responsibility for their initiation and consequences upon yourself.
- You have the right to offer no reasons or excuses to justify your behaviour.
- You have the right to judge if you are responsible for finding solutions to other people's problems.
- You have the right to change your mind.
- You have the right to make mistakes—and be responsible for them.
- You have the right to say, 'I don't know'.
- You have the right to be independent of the goodwill of others before coping with them.
- You have the right to be illogical in making decisions.
- You have the right to say, 'I don't understand'.
- You have the right to say, 'I don't care'.
- You have the right to say no, without feeling guilty.

These rights were manifested in techniques such as 'broken record' (continuing to say the same thing until you get what you want) and 'fogging' (moving the subject away from the other person's point and bringing it back to yours).

The 1970s

By the 1970s, mainly in America, the women's movement was taking up assertiveness, and developing a wide range of techniques to suit the specific situations which women faced in their daily lives. Their processes were simple, and gave a range of solutions for differing situations.

By the end of the 1970s assertiveness was well established as a means of training, particularly for women in America and in the UK. Courses were run publicly on low budgets, so that many women could attend, and were also run inside organizations, particularly when these organizations had a commitment to developing women.

Men also found the techniques useful, and programmes were run for mixed groups as well as women-only groups. Fewer programmes were for men only.

The 1980s

In the 1980s there was a substantial spread of courses throughout the UK. Training was also being offered to trainers to run assertiveness courses.

The 1980s saw the beginnings of a shift from the techniques-based approach to a more internalized approach. The original 1970s techniques were often seen as being 'bolted on' to existing skills with little change, if any, to the feelings inside. The techniques were often over-used and, as a result, gave assertiveness a poor reputation, as the behaviour ended up being aggressive instead of being assertive. Assertiveness often became associated with manipulation and tricks; many people became, and many still are, wary and cynical about assertiveness. Some dictionaries contribute to the confusion by describing assertiveness as being strident and determined to achieve your own rights. In the *Concise Oxford Dictionary* alone there is a diversity in the definition of assertiveness. For the word 'assert', there are three streams of meaning (COD, 1990):

declare or state clearly
insist on one's rights or opinions, demand recognition
vindicate a claim

whilst 'assertive' brings in additional meanings such as:

tending to assert oneself
forthright
positive
dogmatic

and the definition of self assertion is:

the *aggressive* promotion of oneself (our italics)

These definitions are possibly linked to the ways in which assertiveness was taught in the early days. More recent thinking on assertiveness distances assertiveness from aggression, and moves away from a technique base to the more recent ways of working with assertiveness that have evolved into the 1990s.

Despite the difficulties about the approach, assertiveness has spread within organizations. Programmes are run for men as well as women, and assertiveness has been introduced as a subject on many personal development, management, and communication programmes.

In the UK, Ken and Kate Back (Back, Back and Bates, 1992) shared their experience of working with managers inside organizations. They used 'assertion' to refer to behaviour that involves:

- standing up for your own rights in such a way that you do not violate another person's rights
- expressing your needs, wants, opinions, feelings and beliefs in direct honest and appropriate ways

They continued that:

... assertiveness is based on the *beliefs* that in any situation:

- you have needs to be met
- you have rights, so do others
- you have something to contribute; so do others

The aim of assertive behaviour is to satisfy the needs and wants of both parties involved in the situation.

Much of the assertiveness work inside organizations in the UK came directly and indirectly from the detailed advice and analysis of situations outlined by the Backs.

In the same year that the first edition of the Backs' book was published, Anne Dickson first produced her book on assertiveness out of years of experience of working with women (Dickson, 1994). Her ideas were designed specifically to meet the needs of women. From this work stemmed many assertiveness courses for women, both inside organizations and for the general public. Also out of this work came the training of trainers and the Redwood Association for Assertiveness Trainers which is described in the appendix.

In our own work in the 1980s, we increasingly recognized that the technique-based approach was not fulfilling the needs and expectations of people on courses. We recognized that assertiveness needed the involvement of feelings, that the use of assertiveness in one person should not be at the expense of another and that people needed a way of using assertiveness whilst still being themselves. After piloting different approaches on courses, in 1988 we developed a definition and a set of ingredients for assertiveness, rather than a set of techniques. This approach is outlined in more detail in Chapter 2.

The 1990s

The 1990s sees a new wave of assertiveness training where the ability to choose to be assertive in situations comes from people's increased self-esteem and their commitment to endeavour to resolve situations that arise. Although it is still most often found on women's development programmes, there is an increase in the number of general development programmes and managerial development programmes which include assertiveness as an element. Some men are beginning to express an interest in learning assertiveness, usually in a professional context, but often feel it is a weakness to express this interest. For these men, assertiveness as a session or a longer course provides an introduction to the subject. Assertiveness has also become a key part of the content of stress management programmes.

The impression of those who attend assertiveness courses is changing, although in the early 1990s there was sometimes still the lingering impression that assertiveness training was simply about teaching people how to get their own way at the expense of others.

In the continually changing 1990s, there are needs for better, more effective and more flexible communication in all aspects of human relationships. This can be achieved with assertiveness, which will also evolve along with these changing needs.

Trainers are recognizing and meeting the wide variety of needs at all levels inside organizations and in the lives of individuals outside work too. This is discussed further in Chapter 3.

Summary

This chapter introduces the book and sets the scene by briefly describing the development of assertiveness. The key points are:

- assertiveness has evolved in response to changing needs and changing cultures
- assertiveness has links with other developmental theories
- assertiveness has particular application in fast-changing environments and is especially relevant now

References

Back, K. and K. (1992) *Assertiveness at Work*, 2nd edn (with Terry Bates). McGraw-Hill, Maidenhead.

Berne, E. (1964) *Games People Play*. Grove Press, New York.

COD (1990) *The Concise Oxford Dictionary of Current English*, 8th edn. Oxford University Press, Oxford.

Dickson, A. (1994) *A Woman in your own Right*. Quartet, London (first edition 1982).

Harris, T.A. (1967) *I'm OK, You're OK*. Pan, London.

Smith, M.J. (1975) *When I Say No I Feel Guilty*. Bantam, New York.

2 What assertiveness is

Before exploring the relevance of assertiveness in training it is important to be clear about what exactly assertiveness is. This chapter
clarifies assertiveness by looking at:

- assertiveness in comparison with aggression and passivity
- learning to be assertive
- why bother with assertiveness?
- the five ingredients in assertiveness
- the assertive voice
- the relevance of body language and body space

In addition to laying the foundations for further chapters in this book,
everything in this chapter is good raw material when you are running
assertiveness courses, as several of the headings can become sessions or
group discussions.

Definition

What is meant by the word 'assertiveness'? It is especially important to
be clear about the use of the word, as it is often misunderstood and mis-
interpreted and, as shown in Chapter 1, has a range of meaning. Many
people have an opinion on assertiveness and their own understanding
of what it means, which may or may not be correct.

Firstly, assertiveness is a *form of behaviour* and not a personality trait.
Because it is a form of behaviour, it is learnt, and can be learnt, no
matter how helpful or unhelpful people's existing habit patterns may be
to the process of learning. There are glimpses of innate assertive
behaviour when a child around two years of age learns to say 'no', but
this assertiveness is seldom encouraged and is often lost. It then has to
be rediscovered and learned later. Assertiveness should be differentiated
from two other contrasting forms of behaviour: aggression and passivity.

Unlike assertiveness, aggression and passivity are instinctive forms of
behaviour with which people seem to have less difficulty. We have
never heard of anyone attending an aggression course or a passivity
course—although you may know people whom you suspect of having
done so! Most people are pretty good at being aggressive and passive,
but assertiveness comes with more difficulty. Everyone is capable of
behaving in all three ways—aggressive, passive and assertive—but

assertiveness usually presents the biggest challenge and gives the most positive and long-lasting results.

In addition to these three overall broad headings, there are also subtleties and grey areas in between. People who habitually use very aggressive behaviour and who are able to tone it down towards assertive behaviour may experience their own behaviour as being meek, whilst it may actually still be on the verge of aggression.

Equally, people who habitually use very passive behaviour and who are able to move away from this extreme towards assertiveness may feel that their behaviour is rude and overbearing, whilst it is in fact still on the verge of passivity.

Aggression, passivity and assertiveness are all natural forms of behaviour, and there is nothing right or wrong about them—it is a matter of selecting the most appropriate and constructive form of behaviour for any particular situation. Because aggression and passivity usually come easily, we teach assertiveness to give people a choice, a balancing option which is generally accepted to be more constructive and positive than the other two.

Everyone is capable of behaving both aggressively and passively, but most people have tendencies towards one or the other. Equally, everyone is also capable of behaving assertively, but it usually has to be learnt more consciously than the other two.

To define assertiveness, it is helpful initially to clarify what it isn't. It isn't aggression or passivity.

Aggressive behaviour

Aggression means:

- getting your own way, no matter what
- getting your point across at other people's expense
- getting people to do things they don't want to do
- being loud and violent
- being abusive, physically or verbally
- interrupting others
- being intimidating
- winning *at all costs*

This is the stereotype bully—loud, frightening and obvious. If someone attacks you, verbally or physically, you know it's happening. This form of aggression is called *Direct Aggression*, and, although it's frightening, some people find it easier to cope with than *Indirect Aggression*.

Indirect aggression also means:

- getting your own way, no matter what
- getting your point across at other people's expense
- getting people to do things they don't want to do

but it achieves its objectives differently, by:

- being conveyed in a polite, even friendly way
- being quiet and apparently inoffensive
- manipulating or tricking people
- ignoring people
- being silent
- using sarcasm
- using jokes—at other people's expense
- putting people down, making them feel small

Many people find indirect aggression more difficult to deal with, because it's more slippery. An attempt to bring indirect aggression into the open is often responded to with a denial that it's happened:

'You're imagining things'
'You're being neurotic/oversensitive'
'Haven't you got a sense of humour?'
'I never said that'
'You must have misunderstood me'
'It was just a joke'

These two forms of aggression neatly illustrate the importance of remembering that these are forms of behaviour and not personality traits. Quiet, shy people can be just as aggressive as noisy extroverts, they'll simply go about it in a different way.

The overriding motto of aggressive behaviour is: 'Getting my own way, *no matter what*', but underneath aggressive behaviour lies fear and hurt.

The results of aggressive behaviour

The person who relies on aggressive behaviour:

- wins arguments at the expense of others
- gets people's backs up
- is felt to be a persecutor
- is disliked and feared
- gets on by standing on people
- is pompous and overbearing to others
- is seen as wilful and uncaring
- but is really a coward underneath it all

Passive behaviour

Passive behaviour means:

- keeping quiet for fear of upsetting people
- bottling things up
- avoiding conflict, at any cost
- saying 'yes' when you want to say 'no'
- always putting other people's needs first
- not expressing your feelings, thoughts or preferences
- going along with things you don't like or agree with

- apologizing excessively
- inwardly burning with anger, frustration or resentment
- being vague about your ideas and what you want
- justifying your actions to other people
- appearing indecisive whilst really knowing what you want

People who use passive behaviour a great deal can reach the stage where they genuinely do not know what their views or feelings are on a subject, because they've trained themselves not to consider them any more. However, this does not make them serene and calm inside. They may have unfocused feelings of dissatisfaction or resentment at being taken for granted or not taken seriously, but cannot explain or understand why they feel like this.

The overriding motto of passive behaviour is: 'Anything for a quiet life'.

The results of passive behaviour

The person who relies on passive behaviour:

- loses arguments
- is a doormat, at other people's beck and call
- doesn't do what they want or need
- is indecisive
- is a victim (in time would-be rescuers give up)
- is negative, self-pitying
- is lacking in will power
- doesn't get on in life
- may become bitter and resentful in later life

Both aggression and passivity stem from a lack of self-respect, coupled with a lack of respect or excessive respect for others. If there is respect for others along with self-respect, the behaviour that is the manifestation of these inner beliefs is assertiveness: there does not have to be affection for or agreement with the others.

Assertive behaviour

Assertive behaviour is:

- being open and honest with yourself and other people
- listening to other people's points of view
- showing an understanding of other people's situations
- expressing your ideas clearly, but not at the expense of others
- being able to reach workable solutions to difficulties
- making decisions—even if your decision is not to make a decision!
- being clear about your point and not being sidetracked
- dealing with conflict
- speaking up
- having self-respect and respect for other people
- being equal with others whilst retaining your uniqueness
- expressing your feelings honestly but with care
- standing up for yourself

The results of assertive behaviour

The consequences of assertive behaviour are that:

- conflicts are resolved openly
- potentially difficult situations are dealt with early
- confidence increases
- fear reduces as skills are developed in handling emotional situations
- people become equal with others whilst retaining their uniqueness
- there is recognition of the effect of behaviour on others
- people retain their dignity

The definition

Throughout this book and in our assertiveness training we use this definition of assertiveness:

> **Assertiveness is a form of behaviour which demonstrates your self-respect and respect for others. This means that assertiveness is concerned with dealing with your own feelings about yourself and other people, as much as with the end result.**

There are other definitions of assertiveness around, and some assertiveness trainers avoid giving a definition at all. We think it is helpful to have a definition, as it provides a yardstick against which participants and trainer can measure their own assertiveness, and also gives a clear and concise standard to return to during the course, especially if people have become bogged down in the minutiae of a specific situation.

This definition emphasizes the importance of the feelings and thoughts inside and moves away from a bolt-on-technique approach, because assertiveness is not about techniques, special phrases or tricks. Techniques are helpful as tools, but not as an end in themselves.

Our experience is that participants are relieved when they hear this, as a common fear when attending an assertiveness course is that they will become some sort of assertiveness clone, or will be initiated into some secret form of vocabulary and behaviour known only to survivors of assertiveness training!

This definition respects people's individuality and enables each of us to develop our own form of assertiveness which fits our personality and preferences whilst still being effective. Quite the contrary to becoming clones, true assertiveness means that we each are able to become more fully ourselves—sometimes for the first time in our lives.

Participants on assertiveness courses often tell elaborate anecdotes about other people to ask whether their behaviour was assertive or not. It is always impossible to know, because as this definition makes clear, the observed behaviour is only on the surface—the test of assertiveness can only be if we were to know what *feelings* were being experienced inside.

For example: Steve had, for 20 years, been a store manager with a large retailer. He was well liked by his staff, effective, and carried an air of jovial good humour around him. He had a reputation for being easy-going and for always being the person who would rescue the store from a crisis: 'Good old Steve' who could be relied on to cope with everything, and to whom everyone turned when they had their own personal crises. On the surface, Steve appeared confident, capable and assertive. Until one day when Steve snapped, had a severe nervous breakdown, and, a shattered man, was found a low-key quiet job to tide him over until retirement.

Steve had habitually been using passive behaviour for over 20 years. Behind the calm, confident exterior was a man full of rage, anger and bitterness at the way everyone took him for granted and walked all over him. The only way he'd known how to cope was to bottle all his feelings up, go along with what everyone else wanted and fool himself as well as others into believing that he was all right.

Steve's case demonstrates how dangerous it is to attempt to diagnose other people's behaviour. Trainers on assertiveness courses, of course, have to deliver judgements on the participants' experiments with behaviour. Fortunately, in the course room, you can stop and ask people how they're actually feeling. They may not tell you the truth. They may not tell themselves the truth, but at least you can ask the question.

In addition to knowing the feelings being experienced, the other yard-stick for diagnosing assertiveness is by knowing the intention behind the behaviour.

For example: a quick quip can wound very deeply and be perceived by its recipient as being very aggressive. It may have been intended to be humorous and have been delivered with love. Only in an ensuing assertive conversation will the true intention become clear. This does not, however, invalidate the recipient's hurt.

Learning to be assertive

Assertiveness is a simple concept to learn in theory, but most people have difficulty when they try to put it into practice. Some people find it easier than others to put assertiveness into practice, and still fewer seem to behave naturally in an assertive way. However, beware of the person who proudly tells you that they do not need assertiveness training, as their boss/partner/children/colleagues are constantly remarking that they are 'quite assertive enough already'. Almost always this unfolds to reveal aggressive behaviour, from which the other parties involved bear the scars.

Why do we have consciously to learn assertiveness when most of us have so little trouble with aggression and passivity? Some of the answer lies in the conditioning and culture within which we were brought up. This book reflects the fact that our experience is mostly in the United Kingdom, where vestiges of Victorian upbringings and our ideas of what constitute acceptable behaviour collude against assertive behaviour. Our experience of training assertiveness in other countries and with people with non-UK backgrounds also reveals the need for assertive behaviour, but often from a different angle.

The influences of culture and conditioning are diverse and subtle. Some of the most immediately relevant are:

- head tapes
- body space and language
- use of vocabulary

Head tapes   The unconscious messages planted in our childhood brains vary from family to family and from person to person. It can be very useful to look at some of the 'head tapes' of which you are aware, from your own upbringing. The term 'head tapes' is used to describe the messages in our heads which operate like small cassette tape loops repeating themselves over and over and influencing our lives. Head tapes are a useful concept to raise on assertiveness courses, as these deeply ingrained messages can often strongly help or hinder people's ability to practise assertiveness. As most people find it a struggle to develop assertive behaviour, bringing their head tapes into consciousness can give them a clearly defined hurdle to overcome.

Here are some common head tapes which encourage non-assertive behaviours:

> 'Don't rock the boat'
> 'Anything for a quiet life'
> 'It's a dog-eat-dog world'
> 'Your elders know best'
> 'Get them before they get you'
> 'Don't be a nuisance'
> 'Don't be big-headed'
> 'Don't be pushed around'
> 'They're all b******s out there'

And so on. As a trainer, it's helpful to become aware of your *own* head tapes and, alongside them, your assumptions about people and the world. Obviously, these will influence your own ability to be a good role model in assertiveness both inside and outside the training room.

The impact of culture and conditioning is strengthened by the power of these conscious and unconscious head tapes.

Body space and   language   The messages conveyed by the use of our bodies and the spaces around them will be interpreted differently, depending on a wide range of factors. Some of the most obvious will be due to the background and upbringing of each person, influenced by country, family, religious, racial and gender roles and interpretations. As physical appearance constitutes 55 per cent of the messages received by others about us (Pemberton, 1984), the accuracy or inaccuracy of the 'de-coding' of these messages strongly influences the possibility of an assertive message getting through. See Figure 2.1, on p. 24.

People brought up in cultures where looking others straight in the eye is seen as offensive may appear to be behaving 'shiftily' and dishonestly to someone from a culture where eye contact is seen as an indication of openness.

The person delivering a perfect assertive script whilst looking threatening or submissive will not be believed. And trainers whose body language convey messages contrary to their voice may create confusion in the course participants or at worst, cynicism.

Use of vocabulary This is not only the use of different languages but colloquialisms and dialect differences which are interpreted differently depending on our upbringing and understanding.

For example: a person on an assertiveness course in the West Country found being addressed as 'my love' in shops, deeply offensive, sexist and patronizing, while people brought up in the area were unaffected and unoffended.

Recent research (Tannen, 1991) also shows that gender has a significant influence in the way in which words are translated, because men and women (sometimes consciously but mostly unconsciously) use conversation and words differently.

To give a very general example: women use words and conversation to build links, so a woman will look for, and appreciate, words and phrases which emphasize similarities between her and the other person. Meanwhile, men use words and conversation to demonstrate their independence of thought and action, and so value words and phrases which emphasize how different they are from the other person. This may explain why women often complain that their male friends or partners do not seem interested in what they've been doing, whilst men complain that their female friends or partners 'go on' in unnecessary detail.

Of course, there is more to it than this general example. There are several books on the market on this subject and they are well worth reading as they have direct relevance to assertiveness.

Fight or flight syndrome In addition to conditioning and culture, our human biology also works against assertiveness. Our bodies are designed to help us in stressful and dangerous situations by automatically triggering the release of hormones to enable us to either fight or run away with seemingly superhuman energy. Many people tell of surviving appalling accidents by miraculously being able to run away from the scene, only to discover later that they had serious fractures or wounds, or of finding seemingly superhuman strength to rescue a trapped friend or relative. This physical response is commonly referred to as the 'fight or flight' syndrome and it manifests itself in many different ways, such as raised pulse rate, heart pounding, feeling sick, fainting, sweating, mind going blank, trembling knees, and so on.

'Fight or flight' is an essential survival tactic for living in the wild, where continued existence depends on being able either to fight and slay predators, or to run away with exceptional speed. Although our society has changed so dramatically since those days when we all lived in the wild, our bodies have not. Our instinctive response to difficult situations is still either to fight (aggressive behaviour) or to run away (passive behaviour).

While fighting or running away might have been good tactics in the Stone Age they aren't necessarily the most effective way to deal with situations in the late twentieth century! However, it does explain why people don't seem to need courses on aggressive or passive behaviour—they just come naturally.

Concerns about assertiveness

All these factors conspire, in varying intensities, against individuals' abilities to behave assertively and for their behaviour to be interpreted accurately by others. On assertiveness courses it is a useful early exercise, having defined assertiveness, to ask participants why they don't already behave assertively. They usually come up with:

> 'It seems selfish'
> 'It seems rude'
> 'If I'm in an intimate relationship, the other person should just know what I think without me saying'
> 'People should accept me as I am'
> 'I can't say a straight "no"—it seems so abrupt'
> 'It will take longer'
> 'I don't know how to'
> 'They should guess what I feel—why should I spell it out?'
> 'It seems frightening to talk about feelings'
> 'I don't want to offend people'
> 'If people don't understand me, it's their problem'
> 'I don't want to make a fool of myself'
> 'We don't talk about things like that in our family'

Think about which of these, and which others, apply to you.

If there are all these difficulties to overcome for most people, then why should they bother to put themselves through the process of learning assertiveness? What's the benefit to you, as a trainer, to you as a person, and to the people coming on your courses?

Why bother with assertiveness?

On courses, the answer to this question varies enormously from person to person. It also depends greatly on which other forms of behaviour the person most often uses. Responses from participants vary from the general:

> 'I want to stand up for myself more'
> 'Improved communications'
> 'Less misunderstandings'
> 'Get what I want more often'
> 'I don't want to be taken for granted any more'
> 'I want to be able to sort things out without losing my temper so often'

to the specific, such as:

> 'I want to talk to my girlfriend about her parents coming at Christmas without it becoming a major row'
> 'I want to be able to take things back to shops'
> 'I want to stop my ex-boyfriend making obscene phone calls to me'
> 'I don't want my sister to take me for granted any more'
> 'I don't want my next door neighbour to keep parking in my space'

You'll be able to think of many other reasons why people bother with assertiveness. To demonstrate further the detrimental effects which can occur on a personal level with the use of aggression and passivity, we use the concept of gathering 'notches'. Other trainers use the concept of 'stamp collecting' in the same context. Both metaphors make the same point.

Picture yourself on a day when, although you start off feeling neutral, after a while you begin to feel not too good about yourself, and therefore are not assertive. A series of events, if not dealt with, can build up notches of anger, frustration and hurt, over a period of time. It could be a day, a week, a year or even several years.

For example: on arrival at your office, you are about to reverse into the only remaining parking space, when someone else slips past you into the space. About to give the driver a piece of your mind, you discover that she is the new divisional director on a visit. As your pay review is due, you decide to drive around the block several times to find an alternative space instead.

Having reached your office, late, you discover that the course administration has gone wrong and the handouts for today's course are not ready. The course administrator is very upset at her oversight so it doesn't seem the right moment to have a go at her.

You struggle through a course attended by people who are under threat of redundancy and who decide to take out their venom about the company on you. You really don't feel up to dealing with 10 angry people for whom you feel sympathy.

And so on and so on. You can invent your own situations to add to the list! The point is that, in each of these situations, the person involved has some choice but, for various reasons, chose not to deal with the situation and used passive behaviour to avoid doing so.

The situation may have passed but the feelings of anger, frustration, indignation, hurt or whatever do *not* pass. Each piece of feeling is another click up on the ratchet—a little notch of bottled-up feelings. Multiply this over a period of days, weeks or even years, and you are ripe for explosion.

So maybe: after several weeks of this, your partner might mention, quite mildly, that he or she isn't very keen on your new sweater. And wham! The weeks of bottled-up frustration, hurt and resentment come blasting out in anger—a pendulum swing from passivity to extreme aggression.

Most people find these explosions of aggression very cathartic, ridding them of all the rubbish they've collected over the weeks. But sadly it may be very damaging to their relationship with the person on the receiving end. This isn't assertiveness, this is dumping!

And whilst there may be a high of elation clicking the ratchet right down, it can often be temporary, followed by remorse, shame or embarrassment: 'I didn't really mean to say/do that.' But the damage has been done.

These explosions can be so damaging that their owners may overcompensate and retreat again into passive behaviour until the ratchets notch up enough pressure for another.

Of course, this is an extreme scenario, to make the point, but it will seem familiar to most of us. It illustrates the damage that can be done by someone behaving passively until an aggressive explosion. For the individual, this is physically placing a lot of stress on them; either using energy keeping things bottled up, or using energy exploding. Equally, the person using aggressive behaviour in every situation is using up huge amounts of energy in being 'clippy', sarcastic, manipulative, or openly verbally or physically violent.

Dealing with situations assertively reduces (if not totally eliminates) those notches on the ratchet. By dealing, if possible, with each situation at that time and with the relevant person, it increases (although doesn't guarantee) the chances of people feeling better about themselves, and *feelings* are what assertiveness is all about.

Choices in assertiveness   When people first come across assertiveness, they often are fearful that we are suggesting that they should use assertive behaviour, and that their other behaviours are in some way inferior or wrong.

Behaviour cannot be judged to be helpful or otherwise in a vacuum.

There is nothing wrong with aggression or passivity—in many situations they are the most helpful and appropriate behaviours.

For example: a participant on an assertiveness course spent two days rehearsing her assertive response to a man in her office who consistently belittled her and any suggestions she had for more effective ways of working. On her return to the office she tackled him assertively about this, and maintained an assertive response to him over the following weeks. All to no avail. He was simply not listening or taking in what she was saying or doing.

One evening, when they were having a social drink in the pub before travelling home, the man continued to belittle her in front of her colleagues. In frustration, she poured his pint of lager over his head and stormed out of the pub. The man pursued her, asking 'What have I done?' Amazingly, she managed to compose herself and tell him (yet again) assertively what she thought and felt about his behaviour. This time it worked, but it had taken the pint of lager to gain his attention!

So sometimes aggression is the most helpful form of behaviour, while sometimes it's appropriate to keep quiet. Assertiveness is not a form of behaviour for all situations—imagine how boring it would be if we all behaved in exactly the same way all the time—but it is the most constructive form of behaviour most of the time, and especially in tricky situations where the outcome is important or there is a high risk of misunderstanding.

As most of us are pretty skilled at passive and aggressive behaviour, learning assertiveness gives us a third option.

The five ingredients

Having clarified what assertiveness is, why it is a *learnt* behaviour and why any of us might bother with it, we enter the area of how to do it. There are probably as many techniques of assertiveness as there are exponents so, to avoid confusion, it's really important to keep them in perspective and remember that they are merely a means to an end. People usually worry a great deal about getting the techniques right and forget that the overall goal is in the definition, i.e. to develop self-respect and respect for others.

It is helpful to refer to the 'ingredients' in assertiveness rather than 'steps'. Steps can become mechanical and occasionally meaningless and unworkable, while thinking of 'ingredients' gives the person more scope to convey their message in their own way. As long as all the ingredients are in there, it's still assertive.

There are also no set phrases, trick techniques or magic words, which is often disappointing news to people who've only enrolled on an assertiveness course to have a form of secret vocabulary revealed to them!

The five vital ingredients are (Willis and Daisley, 1994)

1 Listen
2 Demonstrate that you understand the other person
3 Say what you think and feel
4 Say specifically what you want to happen
5 Consider the consequences for yourself and others of any joint
   solutions

1 Listen   Being a good listener is a key part of assertiveness. Listening well does not mean agreeing or becoming passive. Listening well is usually easier if you like people or what they are saying. It can be more difficult to remain open to what they are saying when:

- the other person is waffling
- you disagree with it
- the other person is expressing very strong feelings
- you experience the other's behaviour as aggressive
- there are distractions
- your mind wanders to other things
- you are busy thinking about what you are going to say
- you've had difficulties with this person before
- the subject is complex or controversial
- you have strong feelings about the subject or person

As assertiveness is often about sorting out difficult situations and mis-understandings, listening comes first as a key skill.

This may appear obvious, but many people are poor listeners without realizing it. In assertiveness it's important to listen not only to the actual words being spoken, but also to listen to the feelings underlying the words and the intent resulting from them. Sometimes, simply to give people the space to express their views and really to listen well to them is enough to defuse the situation.

If assertiveness is about self-respect and respect for others, then the minimum respect people can give each other is at least to hear them out, and most people are pretty good at knowing when others are feigning attentive listening. Not being listened to creates negative feelings and thoughts such as:

embarrassed	angry
silly	irritated
'I must be boring'	outraged
hurt	'how dare they!'
inadequate	frustrated
self-conscious	indignant
foolish	

It's interesting to note how these common reactions to not being listened to are usually instant, and polarize into a passive response (column on the left) or an aggressive response (column on the right). In this way, simply by not listening sufficiently the effectiveness of the communication has already deteriorated.

Again, there is evidence that gender also has an influence in the ways in which people demonstrate that they are listening.

For example: in general, when women listen, they given small nods of encouragement backed up by 'mmm's' or small words of support. In contrast, when men listen, they stay still and silent.

So it's hardly surprising that there are so many misunderstandings, as the men assume, wrongly, that the women's nods mean agreement, whilst the women assume, wrongly, that the men aren't listening, so start to repeat themselves. All the more need for assertiveness!

2 Demonstrate that you understand

This ingredient is precise and important to understand, as many people have been on courses or learnt techniques in which they're taught the importance of empathizing with the other person. However, unless this is done well, it can easily become patronizing and worthless and people on the receiving end can feel manipulated.

Participants on courses often tell us of the latest symptom of this mis-understanding, which seems to go in fashions. Some popular attempts at demonstrating understanding which fail spectacularly include statements like:

> 'I hear what you're saying'
> 'I know where you're coming from'
> 'I understand exactly how you feel'

There are no trick phrases in assertiveness, and the examples above are usually greeted with hoots of derision. Sadly, phrases like these can contribute to scepticism about assertiveness generally.

If there are no set phrases, what do you say? We emphasize the word 'demonstrate' because this requires more than just words. To demonstrate that you understand, you could:

- Summarize your understanding of the other person's feelings. This enables them to correct you if you've got it wrong.
  For example: 'You are obviously feeling very angry about this' might enable the response: 'No, it's more hurt than anger'.
- Summarize what you understand the other person to have said, as in: 'So my absence on Thursday means that you've been unable to complete your report and now you're feeling under pressure?'
- Give a parallel example from your own experience to check that you've understood them properly, as in: 'When my father was ill, I was devastated even though it was expected, so it must be a terrible shock for you to have to cope with this out of the blue'.
- Put yourself in the other person's shoes and try to imagine how they

feel, as in: 'I think I'd feel excited and apprehensive at the same time. Is that how it is for you?'

- Ask a straight question, as in: 'Are you confused about this?'

All of these build bridges with the other person and let them know that you've taken the time and trouble to consider them. The more highly charged the situation, the more important this ingredient is. A lot of heat can be immediately taken out of a situation by getting this right.

What if you *don't* understand? Then say so. In which case your opening remark might be along the lines of: 'You seem to be very upset about this but I don't really understand why. Can you explain a bit?'

3 Say what you think and feel

People accustomed to using aggression sometimes have no problems with this one. They can often go on at great length, but sometimes they may not be clear themselves about their feelings—so they just shout! Meanwhile, people who are accustomed to using passivity can have enormous difficulties. This can be because they think that their thoughts and feelings are irrelevant and unimportant, or they may not even be aware of what their thoughts and feelings are. This doesn't mean they don't have any, it may simply be because over the years they've trained themselves not to consider them and consequently have lost touch with them. This is often especially so with their feelings.

This ingredient involves taking responsibility for, and being in touch with, your thoughts and feelings. Here there are two cultural habits which are unhelpful. The first blurs the difference between thoughts and feelings. In the UK we often refer to thoughts as feelings, as in: 'I feel that you've got that wrong'. This is a *thought*, not a feeling, despite the 'I feel' in the sentence. Examples of *feelings* are happy, sad, concerned, angry, irritated, and so on. This may seem obvious, but the confusion of thoughts and feelings can be a real stumbling block to people's assertiveness.

The second is the common habit of blaming others for our feelings and not accepting responsibility for them ourselves. This can be seen in sentences which include, 'You make me ...' or 'It made me ...' as in, 'You made me very angry ...' and 'She made me feel a complete fool'.

It is important to challenge this. No one *makes* anyone else feel anything. Our feelings are our own, and there can be a wide range of responses to any common stimulus.

For example: imagine that somebody bursts into your course room whilst you are in the middle of running a course, shouts abuse and rushes out again. There might be many different feelings in response to this intrusion; some people might feel angry, some would be upset, amused, embarrassed, shocked, unaffected, shaken, and so on. The intruder has not *made* anyone feel that way, the feelings are their own. To develop assertiveness this needs to be understood, and people's feelings acknowledged as their own responsibility.

It's important to be as clear as possible with this ingredient, and if it helps, to link it with the event which gave rise to your thoughts and feelings such as: 'I feel really disappointed that you didn't help when you said you would'.

And if you're not sure of your thoughts and feelings, say so; as in: 'I'm not sure how I feel about your remarks', or 'I'm rather confused about the situation'.

4 Say specifically what you want to happen

The emphasis on the word 'specifically' is because dropping hints doesn't work and people are not generally telepathic! Being clear about what you want to happen increases the chances of it happening and decreases the possibilities of misunderstandings.

Many people think that having covered the other ingredients it must be obvious what outcome they want, but it isn't necessarily obvious to anyone else, so make it clear and specific.

People on courses often protest at this, saying, 'They ought to know what I want'. That may be your view, but the reality is that most people won't know unless you tell them. The content here will depend entirely on your own objectives in having the conversation, and takes both of you into the future: 'I'd like you to stop it immediately'. 'I want this on my desk on Friday', 'I don't want to have to sort this out again'.

Ingredients two, three and four may seem, initially, a very cumbersome way of getting your message across, but not necessarily. Assuming you've listened well, they can slot together neatly, as in: 'You seem upset about this, but I'm confused and would like you to explain a bit more.'

Or with the ingredients in a different order: 'I'm disappointed that you're not trying the role play. You obviously feel strongly about it but I'd still like you to have a go'.

In a perfect world, you express what you want to happen and the other person agrees—mission accomplished!

As it doesn't always neatly happen like that there is a further, fifth, ingredient to use when you're stuck.

5 Consider the consequences of joint solutions

A joint solution is not a compromise. Compromise means meeting half-way, and often no one is fully satisfied with the outcome. Considering the consequences of joint solutions might involve a longer conversation, but results in a solution with which both of you agree.

Considering the consequences means exploring the acceptability of various options as in: 'How would it be for you if . . . ?', 'What about . . . ?', 'Would it be better for you if . . . ?', 'What if . . . ?'.

As a result of this exploration and lateral thinking, you may discover a solution which neither of you had previously considered and which is quite different from a compromise.

It does require commitment to find a joint solution, and might need some persistence. However, this time and energy is well spent when it results in a lasting solution with which you both agree.

If all this is beginning to sound rather technique-based, keep the definition in the back of your mind and remember that assertiveness is primarily about your feelings about yourself and the other person.

An assertive voice

Getting assertive words together in your head is one thing, delivering them assertively is another! It's possible to deliver a perfectly assertive 'script' in a sarcastic or tentative tone of voice to create a totally different impression. Research by Albert Menrabhain (see Pemberton, 1984) revealed that the percentage contribution to the total message we convey is as shown in Fig. 2.1. The words—your assertive script—are just the beginning, as they form only 7 per cent of the total message conveyed. To ensure that they remain assertive, you must *sound* assertive and *look* assertive whilst delivering them.

Words

This means what we actually say, rather the way in which we say it. Of course any words can be said in an aggressive, passive or assertive way, but there are some tendencies in either the number of words or the types of statements which are likely to be attributed to each of the three types of behaviour. Here are some statements typical of each of the three types of behaviour:

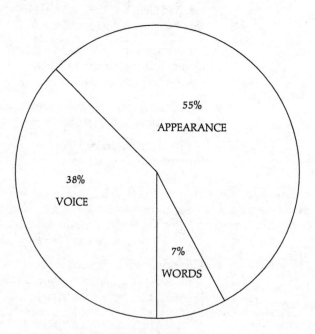

Figure 2.1   *Contributions to a total message*

Words when someone is being aggressive

The types of statements that are made when people are being aggressive tend to emphasize their importance. So when phrases are spoken the 'I' is usually stressed giving excessive emphasis on their own situations, making threats in statements, questions and requests which make them difficult to say no to, and praising themselves at the expense of others. For example:

Excessive emphasis:

'I'm right'
'*My* view is ...'
'*I* think, *I* know'
'I know best'
'*You* need to ...'
'*You* ought to, *you* must ...'
'*Everybody* should ...'
'They mustn't'

Threatening questions, statements and requests

'If you don't get that done today, I will be furious'
'You had better do it or else'
'Why on earth did you do it that way? My way was much better'
'Can't you see what a mess you're making?'
'Can't you understand? Are you stupid?'
'I don't suppose you've done it yet?'
'You'd better get it right next time or you're for it'

Praising self or criticizing others

'This is easy, you know'
'I can't see why you are having problems with it'
'I don't have problems with that'
'You've made a right mess of that'
'I should have done it myself'
'It's your fault'
'It works when I do it'

Aggressive behaviour is conveyed with a voice which is:

- fast
- blustering
- pompous
- loud
- strident
- sharp
- abrupt
- shouting
- clipped
- sarcastic
- cold

- hard
- sneering

The first few adjectives on this list tend to accompany direct aggression whilst the last few tend to accompany indirect aggression.

Words when someone is being passive

Statements and questions will have some or all three of the following general characteristics and the words will show patterns similar to the following examples:

Long-winded and with extra words

> 'You know what I mean'
> 'Maybe. Perhaps, possibly'
> 'Sort of, kind of, you know'
> 'Well, only, only if . . .'
> 'Er, um ah . . .'
> 'I don't mean to interrupt, but could you possibly . . .'
> 'Would it be all right, that is if you have time, and you don't mind, that is to say could you . . .?'

Apologies and justifications

> 'I'm very sorry, oh, I'm so sorry'
> 'I wouldn't normally mention it and I'm ever so sorry to bother you now but could I just possibly speak to you about . . .'
> 'I never meant to'
> 'I hope you don't mind, but . . .'
> 'Please forgive me'
> 'I wouldn't normally mention it, but . . .'
> 'Sorry, but everyone else says so too'
> 'It isn't me that says so'

Self-criticism or putting yourself down

> 'I don't always get it right, so I expect you're right'
> 'I'm no good at this'
> 'Don't expect me to do well'
> 'I usually make mistakes'
> 'You go first, you're more important'
> 'I'm probably wrong, you're probably right'
> 'Don't take any notice of me, I really don't know what I'm talking about'
> 'I should have, I ought to have'
> 'Don't take any notice of me'

Passivity is also conveyed with a voice which is:

- soft
- hesitant
- tentative
- with little expression or emphasis

- trailing off at the end of sentences
- ending in tears or an apology
- slow
- quiet
- fast and garbled
- whispering

Words when someone is being assertive

Statements and questions when people are being assertive are clear and open. They encourage open responses from the other person and do not excessively praise or diminish the speaker or the other person. For example:

Openness to others

'What do you think?'
'How do you feel about that?'
'Tell me more about your idea'
'How does this fit in with your ideas or plans?'
'Let's look at it from both our points of view'

Clear, to-the-point statements with no particular emphasis on the 'I'

'I prefer, I'd like, I feel, I think'
'My experience is ...'
'I think this because ...'
'I will undertake to ...'
'I am not sure so let's ...'

Constructive criticism and suggestions

'How about?'
'Would you like to?'
'Let's look at all the options'
'When you interrupt me I feel annoyed, I'd prefer ...'
'Yesterday I was confused when you explained this. Will you go over the last section again?'
'Right now I need time to think. Can we take a break?'

Assertive behaviour is conveyed with a voice which is:

- steady
- firm
- warm
- clear
- sincere
- neither loud or soft
- audible
- varied tone

All aspects of the voice contribute to this impression. So in addition, consider:

- speed of delivery
- dialect or accent
- volume
- pitch

Body language and space

Body language

Your voice together with your words contributes 45 per cent of your total message, but the major part is in your appearance. Everyone is an expert in body language—we read it consciously and unconsciously every day—and people either know consciously when they are receiving a mixed message or get confused. So it is no use delivering your training (especially if it is on assertiveness!) whilst shuffling your feet, fiddling with your watch strap and looking anxiously round the room!

However, an accurate meaning cannot be read from one gesture or posture alone so body language has to be taken in its entirety. For example, folded arms could mean aggression—'I'm not letting you near me', passivity—'Please don't come near me, I'm scared', or it might simply mean that the people are cold or covering up a stain on their clothing! Do not be lured into passing judgement on one gesture in isolation. Nevertheless, in terms of the three behaviours, here are some clues:

Aggressive behaviour is conveyed by

- staring
- leaning back with hands behind head
- pointing fingers, pencils, etc
- clenched fists
- clenched jaw
- taking up maximum space
- fingers drumming

Passive behaviour is conveyed by

- little or no eye contact
- looking down or to one side
- expressionless
- sad or fearful expression
- body shrinking in and down
- shoulders up
- rounded shoulders
- taking up very little space
- nervous smile
- legs wrapped around each other

Assertive behaviour is conveyed by

- direct eye contact without staring
- shoulders back
- upright posture
- open hand and arm movements
- relaxed
- expression on face fitting feelings being expressed
- taking up appropriate amount of space
- sitting and standing upright

There are, of course many refinements on all of these, and they have to be seen in context.

Body space   Also linked with appearance is body space. Aggression can be conveyed simply by standing so close as to become threatening or oppressive. Equally, it's difficult to have an in-depth conversation with someone if they persist in standing too far away.

On day-to-day terms, we feel comfortable with some people close to us whilst we may prefer others to keep their distance. Allan Pease describes these distances as 'zones' or portable 'air bubbles' which we each have around us (Pease, 1981).

- **Intimate zone, 15–45 cm** This is the most important as it is this zone that people guard as if it were their own property. Only those who are emotionally close enough are permitted to enter it. This includes lovers, parents, partner, children, close friends and relatives. There is also a sub-zone that extends up to 15 cm from the body, which implies physical contact.
- **Personal zone, 46 cm–1.22 m** This is the distance that we stand from others at parties and social functions.
- **Social zone, 1.22–3.6 m** We stand at this distance from strangers, the carpenter doing repairs, the postman, new employees at work and people whom we do not know very well.
- **Public zone, over 3.6 m** Whenever we address a large group of people, this is the comfortable distance at which we choose to stand.

The size of the zones depends on the culture in which we're grown up. These zone distances tend to apply to people brought up in countries such as Australia, New Zealand, the UK and North America.

As trainers, it is important to be sensitive to these zones, to recognize that people brought up in other cultures may have different zone distances, and that these often unconscious aspects can make or break our own, and the participants on our courses' attempts at assertiveness.

Summary

In this chapter we have looked at assertiveness in theory and:

- defined assertiveness and its comparison to aggression and passivity
- explored some of the reasons why assertiveness is so difficult including culture, conditioning and the fight or flight syndrome
- suggested some ways in which people benefit from assertiveness
- introduced the five main ingredients of assertiveness
- introduced the importance of the voice, appearance and use of body space in supporting the assertive words.

References

Pease, Allan (1981) *Body Language*, Sheldon Press, London.

Pemberton, Maria (1984) *Effective Speaking*, The Industrial Society, London.

Tannen, Deborah (1991) *You Just Don't Understand*, Virago, London.

Willis, Liz and Daisley, Jenny (1994) *Springboard Women's Development Workbook*, Hawthorn Press, Stroud.

3 The need for assertiveness in training

This chapter examines the key reasons why organizations, individuals and trainers might use assertiveness by examining the needs of each group and the ways in which assertiveness meets these needs. In the many different theories of organizations and learning and development there are common denominators which point to the need to develop skills of assertiveness. The main areas examined relate to the changes taking place at an ever-increasing speed around us today. Changes in:

- the nature of the society
- the nature of organizations
- the relationship between organizations and outside world
- styles of leadership and management
- the style of one-to-one communication
- the nature of training and the move towards individuals' responsibilities for their own development

The chapter concludes with five case studies of organizations which use assertiveness training.

Changes in society

The rate of change in our society has speeded up substantially with the development of science, technology and world trade. Recession has also meant coping with change and using fewer people to do the same amount of work. Today people may be either invigorated or overwhelmed by the speed with which world events happen and are communicated. Technological innovation has changed the nature of work and leisure time. Scientific discoveries and explorations bring solutions to many problems but also raise more questions, particularly moral ones.

We now live in a world of satellite links which beam television and telephone messages around the world in seconds. In the 1890s people waited weeks or months to hear news of war or developments. In the 1990s TV reporters in remote parts of the world send pictures of events as they are happening and converse with news presenters 'on air'.

Robotics have transformed many production lines, and the reductions in the labour force predicted a decade or two ago are now a reality. The technology of 'virtual reality', in which computers generate pictures that people can enter into and interact with, is now available. Its uses are apparently limitless: for instance, it enables architects to change design specifications, view buildings from above, underneath, inside, outside, left side, right side, and also enables medical researchers to generate a mock-up of the internal organs of the body. Interactive pornography is also being developed.

Changes in organizations

Inside organizations the pace of change has quickened and continues to move faster and faster, decreed by the changes in society, in the economy, and technology. The changes in demographics, working patterns, and the move from hierarchical structures to flatter, more project-based structures demand more informal relationships between managers and staff and a greater reliance on good relationships across the organization. More and more organizations are contracting work out, which means dealing with subcontractors on a scale hitherto unknown. These changes place demands upon organizations in relation to:

- communications
- power
- pressures for balance between work and social life
- equal opportunities and changing culture

To extend the link to assertiveness training, imagine the costs in real terms to organizations of wasted money, lost sales and wasted time, when uncooperative colleagues hold up production or information, work is undertaken by slower or less effective processes, work is done unnecessarily and so on. All of these situations could be resolved quickly and effectively with assertiveness. The cost of lack of assertiveness can be very high indeed and can extend all the way from two shopfloor workers who sabotage each others' work because of an unresolved conflict to board directors who don't iron out difficulties between them and leave their two departments struggling to get sufficient information to function effectively.

Communications

Many key writers point to the changes that are needed in the nature of communications and in relationships. John Harvey-Jones, ex-chairman of ICI, believes (see Harvey-Jones, 1988) that:

The next prerequisite with a switched-on organisation is perhaps the most difficult to achieve in a British environment, and this is openness of communication.

and later he continues:

We have to have a far greater tolerance of difference and a far greater respect for differences of view.

Both these statements point to key parts of assertiveness, namely openness and honesty, and respect for others.

Charles Handy's predictions about the future of work (Handy, 1985) are now mostly a reality. 'Hierarchies' and 'bureaucracies' are on the way out and 'networks' and 'partnerships' are growing. He further predicted (Handy, 1990) the growth of a flexible labour force which comprises approximately one quarter of the paid workforce.

If you add to the flexible labour force all the self-employed, who are mostly in the contractual fringe or organisations, you will find that over one third of Britain's paid workers are not actually in conventional full-time jobs. The way things are going it may well be that there will be more people working *outside* the core than *inside* it by the end of the century.

More recently, Handy (1994) indicates the need to understand the importance of investment in intelligence, identifying nine types of intelligence:

- factual
- analytical
- linguistic
- spatial
- musical
- practical
- physical
- intuitive
- inter-personal

He describes inter-personal intelligence as

the wit and the ability to get things done with and through other people.

Combine this with his belief that:

Life will be unreasonable in the sense that it won't go on as it used to; 'We shall have to make things happen for us rather than wait for them to happen'.

and it is clear that assertiveness will be needed to bring order to the confusion which will undoubtedly arise.

The projected and current changes in organizations mean that more people will be placed in situations where their most effective means of influencing others will be through inter-personal skills and this will mean becoming better at being assertive in a wide range of situations. Barham and Rassam (1989) emphasize this too. Sir John Egan at Jaguar states

Managers in the future will be judged in two ways. Firstly, how good are they in their job? Secondly, how good are they in a project team or task force?

These trends in organizations mean more reliance on greater and more effective communication. More contract working and self-employment mean that colleagues and staff working on projects who are operating on a freelance basis will contract in and out on specific pieces of work, will have a greater say in setting their own terms and conditions of work and, depending on the state of the economy, will drive harder or easier bargains.

Barham and Rassam (1989) indicate that

Managers in the future will have to manage an increased and more diverse range of lateral relationships including those with managers from different functional areas.

People now need to develop effective working relationships very quickly. They are no longer able to spend years getting to know each other.

Power in organizations

These changes in the structures and processes of organizations mean that relationships will vary enormously from stable and fairly permanent to very flexible and temporary. Managers will have to work from positions of personal authority earned through respect in their relationships with others rather than through formal authority vested in them through their job description. Individuals will increasingly find themselves relying more on their inter-personal skills than on other forms of influence in relationships.

Margaret Ryan identified four forms of power or influence which operate inside organizations (Ryan, (1986):

- **Formal authority** The right to make decisions, conferred on you by higher management. It depends on people's acceptance of your right to decide, and is seldom sufficient on its own but is usually found in conjunction with one or more of the other types of power.
- **Expertise** Specialist knowledge and skills, usually acquired through professional training outside the organization. The more exclusive a person's expertise and the more useful it is seen to be in the organization, the more power he or she will have.
- **Resource control** Control of physical, financial or information resources of the organization. People in relatively lowly hierarchical positions can have considerable resource control, but the most power goes to those who control the most valued resources, particularly money and information.
- **Inter-personal skills** The ability to persuade, and to build good relationships. It depends on personal flair, but also on acquired skills through training and practice.

Formal authority doesn't work with contract staff in the same way as it does with employees. If they are self-employed they may fight for their own rights and if employed by a contractor they may see their loyalty as being to the contractor and not to the organization. Interactions are becoming more a matter of discussion, negotiation and assertiveness rather than a question of authority and direction from above.

Pressures on organizations for balance

Increasing emphasis is placed today on the balance between home and work for women and men alike. People expect to have more a fulfilling life outside work and are standing up for what they value and believe in. Senior managers now sometimes refuse promotions or transfers to other parts of the country or world so that they can spend more time with their family, or so that their children will not have to change schools at crucial examination times. Men and women are refusing or making career moves in relation to their partner's careers.

As Professor Cary Cooper puts it (see Ross and Schneider, 1992):

Forty-year-olds now want to spend more time with their families than those who set the pace in their fifties and sixties. They have seen too many colleagues burnt out or having heart attacks, and they have a healthier attitude to work which is going to make their companies healthier.

Ross and Schneider (1992) indicate:

Balance is the key word. There is a growing realisation of the importance of leisure and time spent outside work to working people's health. Putting in 12-hour days, with long journeys at either end of the day, may help people believe that they are valued and are keeping up with their peers, but this clearly puts a strain on their health. Many people are recognising that it does them and their organisations no good at all if they are constantly under pressure from work.

Again this means that more people will be recognizing the need to influence what is happening on a day-to-day basis at work and wanting to influence the outcomes of decisions to bring about this balance.

Equal opportunities/ changing culture

In the recent past, many organizations have, for sound business reasons, undertaken culture change programmes which involve staff at all levels changing their behaviour towards each other and their customers. The numbers of women entering the labour market is increasing. It is estimated that by 2001, 75 per cent of women of working age will be in work or actively seeking work (Employment Gazette, 1991). Most women's power tends to be based on inter-personal skills, as women have tended in the past to have less formal authority and restricted access to obtaining expertise. Women have also been the main participants on and beneficiaries of assertiveness training and are increasingly bringing such skills into the workplace and identifying needs for more assertiveness training at work.

Some organizations are increasingly seeing that equal opportunities is closely linked to culture change and improved competitiveness in the national and international markets.

Hammond and Holton (1991) identify five sound commercial reasons why equal opportunities is inextricably linked to competitiveness. All of these reasons have inter-personal skills aspects and therefore have implications for assertiveness training. They are:

- **Becoming an employer of choice** Being able to choose to attract people who can both cooperate and compete. Making the organization attractive enough through development opportunities, flexible working arrangements and conditions, etc., so that the right calibre of staff will come and stay.
- **The need to get closer to customers** A balanced workforce brings organizations closer to their customers. Customer awareness has increased, whether in large commercial organizations or in small local authorities. Sales and appreciation of services increase as organizations tune in more to their customers' needs. Tuning in takes a balanced approach of respect for the customer and self-respect, both of which are at the core of assertiveness.
- **The costs of imbalance** Hammond and Holton refer to examples of conditions of employment which bring in cost benefits in recruitment and retention terms. They also cite Stuart Crystal, who recruited and trained women to manage the shopfloor because the company believe that the more harmonious relationships which result from employing women managers lead to increased production.
- **The value of differences** The workforce of the future will not be predominantly white and male. 'A varied workforce with people from different backgrounds and experience combined with people able to communicate more openly and effectively leads to a climate where ideas can flourish' (Barham and Rassam, 1989). Women are usually able, at a younger age, to take into account the views of their colleagues and are more sensitive to atmospheres and undercurrents. By age 40, men's skills match those of women. Two of the key ingredients of assertiveness are listening and demonstrating understanding. Both these ingredients improve the skills needed to value differences.
- **The right balance** The commercial advantages of having a balanced workforce are slowly being recognized and as they are, so too may be the advantages of having balance in the communication between all parts of the workforce.

The relationship between organizations and the outside world

Customer care and quality programmes abound as organizations develop their relationship with those who buy their goods and services. Charters propound what the customer can expect by way of good service and demand if service fails to live up to expectations. All of this places demands on the skills of staff. As they deal with increasingly assertive customers, they need to become more assertive themselves.

The concept of 'lean production' (Womack *et al.*, 1990) has implications for substantially more, better and different relationships with suppliers too. It implies, amongst other things, that each organization needs to relate more effectively with its supply chain. Womack *et al.* (1990) indicate clearly that, if we are to bring about the best forms of lean production, organizations need to work towards mutually beneficial ends with their suppliers:

By abandoning power based bargaining and substituting an agreed-upon rational structure for jointly analysing costs, determining prices and sharing profits, adversarial relationships give way to cooperative. Cooperation does not mean a cosy relaxed atmosphere—far from it.

In fact, cooperation requires an open, straightforward assertive atmosphere, leading to joint solutions which find the best courses of action and results for both parties. So there is a demand for working relationships between organizations and the world about them which demands the skills and the results that assertive behaviour can deliver.

This means that managers have to develop their skills and abilities too.

Changes in styles of management and leadership

All the above changes in society, organizations and the relationships between organizations affect and make demands on individual managers and bring substantial pressure to bear on an individual's ability to manage, lead and build successful personal relationships.

Cultural change programmes sometimes include or have as a complementary activity assertiveness training for staff at all levels, particularly more junior staff who in more authoritarian and hierarchical organizations would not have been encouraged to put their views forward. The quality movement also relies heavily on effective communication, particularly upwards. Assertiveness training enables these voices to be heard.

Leaders of the future

Assertiveness also supports the growing trend towards good-quality leadership instead of authoritarian management. As change moves more quickly, in addition to leaders being at the top of organizations, every employed person needs to be able to respond to the situations which face them on a day-to-day basis. To grasp the leadership of a situation involves speaking out, taking a lead and convincing others that the course of action which you are propounding is the most effective and one which will achieve their objectives as well as yours.

To lead to achieve extraordinary accomplishments in whatever field means being able to be assertive with other people. Kouzes and Posner (1987) outline five different ways in which leaders achieve special results:

- **Challenging the process** This means being active, speaking out, standing up to and challenging ideas, systems, procedures, opinions, being the first to do things and taking risks. In assertiveness people are not always going to get their own way but they are more likely to change situations if they are able to say what they think and feel about situations and what they want to happen.
- **Inspiring a shared vision** Breathing life into other people's ideas, hopes and dreams. Not all leaders initiate the idea themselves, so if

leaders are to capitalize on all the creative ideas of those around them and make them happen, they need to listen and be able to speak the language of those around them. Leaders will not be able to light the flame of passion in others unless they are able to convey their own feelings of enthusiasm and interest. Expressing feelings is often the turning point in conversations which changes them from ordinary into assertive conversations.

- **Enabling others to act** Good leaders involve the people who have to live with the results of their decisions in the projects. To do this effectively, everyone involved has to be skilled in assertiveness. Think of projects which you have seen fail or have difficulties. When they are examined with hindsight it is often discovered that a key person or group of people was not committed in the first place but did not speak out at the beginning. Instead, they quietly sabotage good efforts and other times they build up 'notches' of frustration or disagreement until one day they finally blow up; the aggression and bottled-up resentment emerges and only then can it be seen why things have been going wrong. To enable others to act, collaboration and teamwork are essential and both need assertiveness to be effective.

- **Modelling the way** Irwin Federman, President and Chief Executive Officer of Monolithic Memories, speaking at a seminar on corporate excellence says (see Kouses and Posner, 1987):

Your job gives you authority. Your behaviour earns you respect.

Unassertive behaviour can often be tolerated for long periods of time, but it does not gain the best results nor does it show subordinates, bosses or colleagues the way that will succeed in most situations.

- **Encouraging the heart** Means reaching people at the level of their feelings and not simply appealing to their intellect or logic. In their model Kouzes and Posner (1987) talk about recognizing the contributions and rewarding the performance of individuals as well as celebrating successes at the end. Two key ingredients of performance measurement are setting the standards and coaching to achieve them. This demands assertive behaviour so that the standards set are realistic and agreed by both parties. The coaching has to be open and honest and take account of the feelings. And in both cases the results have to be joint solutions, which both sides agree to adhere to and think are reasonable in the circumstances. Compromises will not work and are no good here!

All the above indicate the need for assertiveness inside organizations.

In summary, the benefits to organizations in using assertiveness are:

- less time and money is wasted on ineffective communications
- more effective communication increases profitability
- problems are solved more effectively
- in the long term less time is spent on disputes
- people are clearer about what is needed in given situations

- customers are listened to and joint solutions are more often found
- managers and staff are more likely to get to the truth in a range of situations
- a climate of openness and honesty generates more creativity and innovation when people aren't afraid to speak up
- people speak up to prevent mistakes and make positive suggestions
- information given and received assertively is more accurate
- it promotes development rather than entrenchment in relationships
- true differences are made apparent and recognizable early on
- relationships between individuals and groups are improved
- the responsibility for communication is placed squarely with each individual

Changes in styles of one-to-one communications

The effects of all the changes in society, organizations, leadership and management lead to different responsibilities being placed and different demands being made of individuals in their one-to-one communications. Each individual has more responsibility for communication. It is no longer expected that junior staff wait until asked for ideas on how to work better or feedback on policy and decisions. At all levels people are expected to initiate communication more and to work well within a team.

As things move quickly there is not so much time for people to 'get round to speaking up and speaking out'. Decisions taken and actions agreed can be whisked round the world for implementation in minutes. So the need for 'instant' effective relationships becomes greater. The value of being assertive can be seen in all forms of one-to-one communication orally and in writing, in day-to-day conversations and in formal presentations, in writing memos, letters, training and sales leaflets, electronic mail, proposals and reports.

For example: in one organization where electronic mail was billed as the new, fast, timesaving process, all sorts of problems arose when people took to sending cryptic messages. As a result, people started blaming the system! What was needed to solve the problem was assertiveness training, particularly around the ingredients of assertiveness.

The customer still comes first, but if the customer is being downright rude, or not speaking out enough, assertiveness builds a better, more complete relationship. Good negotiators and salespeople have used assertiveness to improve their results. Assertiveness offers one-to-one communication—as a dynamic and lateral process rather than a linear step-by-step process.

The demands placed on individuals are great. The processes of assertiveness and the skill and energy to continue to apply it are also great, but the resulting benefits are well worth it:

- more difficult situations are resolved
- self-esteem rises

- relationships improve
- assertiveness gives people a process of being more true to themselves
- the assertiveness process enables people to tackle situations which they've had doubts or fears about in the past
- the more often relationships are built on assertiveness the more people can trust that others are telling them what they really think
- assertiveness helps people give and receive positive and negative feedback more easily
- it's less tiring and emotional in the long term
- people command more respect

Moving from training to development

Training is becoming more learner-centred than in the past and much of the design and intention of training now is to give more responsibility to individuals for their own learning. This means that participants on courses need to become more active and proactive rather than passive and reactive. It also implies that trainers have to be able to draw out people behaving passively and cope with the possible lack of reaction and response. As people who've used passivity in the past learn to stand up for themselves more, they often overreact and use aggressive behaviour and this may also need to be dealt with on the course. Personal development plans and training are on the increase, together with a rise in the combination of work and personal development issues being raised on courses.

Assertiveness is a skill which on one level can be learnt fairly mechanically, but on another level can also become a means of personal development, resulting not only in changes in knowledge and skill, but also in changes in levels of effectiveness, attitudes and behaviour. Trainers take more risks in development training than they do in skills-based learning but assertiveness is applicable in both. In *Managing Personal Learning and Change*, Clark (1991) describes the risks which trainers and participants take, and the ways in which people cope with these risks:

The experience of feeling at risk is likely to vary from person to person, but is more certain to arise when:

- an individual takes some action and does not know what the outcome will be
- an individual believes that he or she lacks the resources to cope with a situation.

The range of conditions on any programme where the above can occur are numerous, and can include: introducing yourself or your partner; reporting back on a small-group discussion; asking questions in a large group; taking part in a group exercise or role play; and any feedback activity. Most trainers are aware of risk situations on skills and attitudinal programmes, but it is too easy to assume that what we may see as safe programmes (knowledge-based) or safe parts of programmes can be experienced as high-risk by some learners. One of the problems, in this respect, is that not only is the experience of risk subjective, but also the ways in which we cope with risk are also unpredictable. Such ways may include:

- passivity
- expressing fear, caution and concern for others rather than for self
- expressing confusion or lack of understanding
- asking detailed questions or requesting clarification
- cynicism or hostility
- suspicion or withdrawal
- discounting experiences or compulsive joking
- acting tough or being insensitive
- sarcasm

Although the trainer cannot totally control the risk level in the group, there are three design factors that directly affect the level at any one time. These are: size of group, variety of learning experience, and the time focus of the learning experience.

To this is added a fourth factor—the assertiveness skills of the trainer. All programmes carry a risk and a challenge to the skills of the trainer. Excellent design, professional presentation and material can be wasted if the trainer is not able to handle the unpredictable situations that arise leading to frustration all round.

Case studies— organizations

The five case studies which follow are from a variety of organizations which use assertiveness training for different strategic reasons and in different ways. All the case studies are written by the people concerned in their own words, with an introductory paragraph from us, and give a wealth of useful experience.

Case study

The Macro Group

> **The Macro Group made a conscious decision, with full top management backing, to introduce assertiveness training as part of a proactive training and development strategy. They chose to run mixed-gender courses and involved managers before and after.**

Deborah Smith, Personal and Business Skills Development

The key question for me to answer is 'Why?' Why offer assertiveness training? What benefits does an organization gain? After running in-house courses for more than two years it is interesting to revisit this fundamental question because life without assertiveness training would now be hard to make sense of!

It may help if I briefly sketch the scene in March 1991 when our Managing Director, Harriet Green, asked me to set up a proactive training and development department. I was faced with a potentially ideal (or lethal) platform. There had been no developmental training in the past and my task was to offer relevant training in many new areas. One more slipped on to the agenda would not necessarily arouse special comment. However, I dearly wanted the customers to take this one up. Why?

The observations that lead me to the belief that assertiveness training would be the cornerstone to the success of almost everything else that I wished to introduce were based, quite simply, on my experiences and those of others in the organization. I had been introduced to assertiveness techniques in 1988, during a women's management course. It had often helped me to apply the other techniques that I had been taught (e.g. motivating, delegating) and usually what is common in one person's experience is likely to be true for many others. So when having a post-sales-course discussion with a group of young, articulate women I was staggered to find (when the discussion moved in to the area of 'but my boss says I can't'; 'I can't talk to her because she just bursts into tears') that their perception was 'it is unprofessional to discuss, highlight or otherwise draw attention to the feelings that I have over issues, and equally it is unprofessional for others to do so'. So how did they cope with life at work? Like anyone else choosing to take that path, of course, carrying out their instructions with a greater or lesser degree of agreement, and taking their pent-up emotions home with them, where they would damage home life or health, or we would lose a well-trained individual. Further discussions backed up my initial findings.

I take care not to appear too evangelical about assertiveness. I am, though! How can an individual, or an organization, be truly effective if some part of its available energy is used up in either anger or repressive techniques. How much time is wasted on schemes that are launched with good intentions, but wither because no one wanted to say they didn't agree with the purpose or the process? I won't go on! My aim was to offer plain and practical advice and ongoing support to anyone who chose to take it. My MD had no hesitation in agreeing the proposal and actively encouraged it.

Our company is populated by a greater number of women than men, so initially thoughts of a 'women-only' course were not at the forefront of my mind. I could also see that men's needs were just as valid. Like any trainer, I had to consider whether the course would have more impact if it was run in single-gender groups, but my final decision was not to do this. Our workplace is not single-gender, and the company must benefit from the training. There was a danger that people might be tempted to use their techniques only with people they perceived as understanding them and continuing to avoid the 'real' problem areas. I decided to bite the bullet and invite anyone and everyone to the course. I didn't want it to be marketed as special or different, just something that all contemporary business people need.

The course was advertised with, I believe, simple and practical objectives. The attendance figures show that nearly 90 per cent of the attendees are women, however, which is unrepresentative of the population, but men do attend. I run the courses, which take place over a four-week period, as I am not in favour of 'quick-fix' training. After a lifetime of behaving in a certain way, it takes time for an individual to process the facts about a new technique, let alone believe them and practise them. Therefore, I like the step-by-step approach which allows us to develop ideas gradually, and enables the group (and me) to support and nurture new efforts to apply the learning.

I also favour leading the course personally as I think it is important that I (and therefore the company) am seen as approachable on a range of 'in and out of work' experiences, and that individuals get to hear me talk about my own (sometimes hard to believe now) experiences in the workplace, from domineering bosses to sexual harassment. My approach is candid and explodes many privately held views that 'it's all right for her, I bet she's always been so confident'. It opens up trust and a new dialogue that says to our staff 'we know you are a person and we are interested in what helps and hinders you'. I believe the employers should be seen to roll up their sleeves and deal with the difficult and emotional issues, and not just the ABC items. The release of energy that this can inject into the organization is of utmost importance.

Evaluation takes a standard and a non-standard approach. Delegates evaluate the course for themselves. I also talk to their managers to determine whether any behavioural change has taken place. I offer an ever-open-ear service and, occasionally, use an outside course for those really interested in working with a new group. I would say, however, that the best results are those people that come back to me, sometimes months later, and tell me how they have solved an issue themselves and those that come back and say they feel they would like training (in a different area) as they now feel confident enough to see themselves as deserving of it.

As to drawbacks—well, one or two managers may have taken my name in vain when staff have asked for things that have never been discussed before, but as we are a communicative management team, all my peers were aware of the objectives of the course. They have to screen all applicants and agree their course objectives with them, so there is little room for drawbacks. The main area of difficulty is that of managers nominating staff who they themselves are not managing adequately, and hoping that the course will miraculously address this problem. If I don't spot this when I receive a nomination it always comes out in the first session when we establish the reasons why the individual chose to come on the course. This results in my agreeing, with the delegate, how we will get the manager to have that conversation before the following week. I place great emphasis on this happening and will not move forward with that individual's training until the manager has complied.

I do not yet foresee a time when our company will not offer assertiveness training—maybe when it is taught as part of the general school curriculum we can relax—but until then I believe it should be high on everyone's training agenda.

Case study

**The Woolwich
Building Society**

> **In the Woolwich Building Society the assertiveness courses run have included pre-course work based on a distance learning workbook. The learning experiences from trainers and participants provide useful hints and tips for those starting out on assertiveness training.**

*Jackie Campbell,
Compensation and
Benefits Manager*

The Woolwich Building Society introduced a one-day assertiveness course in 1989, as a result of line manager demand, in the large administration departments within Head Office (e.g. mortgage processing/administration). The initial course dealt with areas such as 'what is assertiveness?', exploring what the delegates felt assertive behaviour is and isn't, skills of assertiveness, e.g. learning how to say 'no', and various role-play exercises. The course was re-examined in 1990 and a distance learning workbook was introduced which was intended as pre-course work and issued around 4–5 weeks before the course date for the delegate to work through. The workbook covers the theory of assertive behaviour, e.g. considering aspects of cultural influences, looking at ways of getting what I want, assertiveness in daily life, etc., with various mini-exercises for the course delegate to reflect on their current attitude and complete with individual responses.

The revamped course naturally drew from the completed workbook and delegates were not as completely new to the topic as they had been previously. The courses were run on an 'as needs' basis and around 4–5 courses with an average of 8–10 delegates were run in the first year. The courses have always been open to both men and women, although the majority of delegates have been women.

The Woolwich approach to training has been for the training adviser (commonly the Training Officer) to be approached by the line manager who either describes the 'problem' or, more commonly, suggests the appropriate training course. Assertiveness training could be the perceived solution for many managers, for example, to solve time-management problems, aggressive or passive behaviour, etc. The training adviser will analyse the situation and will often speak to the individual employee to ascertain the root cause of any perceived problems. In the case of assertiveness training *per se*, individuals would be encouraged to look at alternatives in the open learning centres, e.g. self-help books and interactive video as well as the original workbooks.

Reactions and comments from trainers and delegates about the courses include:

- Mixed courses are useful because they show that men can be under-confident and unassertive as well as women.
- Mixed courses can be prohibitive because this course centres around self-diagnosis and a lot of the perceived lack of assertiveness (especially in the workplace) is actually because of male attitudes, from men who are commonly in a higher grade than the delegate.
- Managers were looking for their staff to be more assertive but didn't like them going back to the office and saying 'no'.
- There was a problem having delegates from the same department on the same course, i.e. perceived lack of confidentiality and inability to discuss specific situations.
- Some managers sent delegates on the course without explaining what the course was or why the individual should attend. This resulted in a very negative attitude from the delegate.

Training advisers felt that in general there was not an attitude of acceptance of the 'new skills' when the course delegate returned to the workplace, i.e. line managers did not feel that they too had to change from an attitude of 'I want this done by whenever' to a more 'let's plan the workload' situation where the employee could reflect on work priorities and pressures and honestly feed back to the manager. This is one aspect of this kind of training or awareness raising that will be considered as part of a new Equal Opportunities Programme which has recently been launched within the Woolwich Building Society.

The whole area of assertiveness and confidence building, especially in clerical and non-management grades, has been highlighted as a major initiative and will form an important part of any package of training. We do not, therefore, see assertiveness training as being able to survive in isolation.

Case study

Littlewoods Home Shopping Division

> **Assertiveness training in the Littlewoods organization arose out of an Equal Opportunities initiative. The courses are aimed at all management grades and include supervisors, although a different strategy has been used for senior managers. Courses are mainly attended by women.**

Janette Fiddaman, Training Manager

One of the first issues any trainer will be faced with when introducing assertiveness training is 'what do you call it?' Allow me to put this into context.

The scenario we faced when introducing our assertiveness training programme was one of a large organization, highly sophisticated in terms of new technology but quite traditional in its approach to management. Previous training tended to concentrate on the hard skills with not a great deal of emphasis or value placed on the soft skills. Obviously times are changing, people's expectations of work relationships are somewhat different now. It is not as acceptable to simply use power and authority as a means of getting the job done. Good interpersonal skills are increasingly important.

The decision to introduce assertiveness training came about as a result of our Equal Opportunity policy. An analysis of the make up of our workforce showed that approximately 80 per cent is female. The majority of middle and senior management posts were held by men, however. An examination of why women were not progressing within the organization revealed a number of reasons including a perceived lack of confidence on the part of women. The decision was made to introduce assertiveness training as part of a positive action programme.

So back to my earlier point, 'What do you call it?' There was quite a lot of pressure to change the title in order to make the topic more acceptable. The advice I would give here is 'be assertive'. What is the point in introducing the concept of assertiveness training if you can't be confident enough to call it what it actually is.

Initially we used external training consultants Liz Willis and Jenny Daisley to pilot the training followed by a 'train the trainer' course, which they ran to train in-house personnel to continue running the programmes.

When we were designing the programme to run in-house the question was raised regarding whether or not to run women-only courses. We initially discussed three options:

- women only
- men only
- mixed gender

The consensus of opinion was to run mixed courses. The training was made available to anyone in management including supervisors. In reality the take-up was mainly lower-middle management. The delegates tended to reflect the composition of the workforce, i.e. 80 per cent female, 20 per cent male.

The objectives of the course were to enable delegates to:

- develop a more open style of management
- develop confidence in dealing with people
- improve communication skills

Evaluation of the programme is a two-stage process. Delegates complete an evaluation form within a few days of completing the course. There is also a follow-up letter sent out 3 months later.

Feedback from the programme has been consistently good. Delegates feel more capable of dealing with difficult situations and difficult people. Generally they are more confident and receptive to the idea of attending other training programmes. The course often has a great impact on individuals.

Assertiveness training forms an integral part of the management training offer. We have been offering this type of training for the last five years and it is now seen as beneficial for staff development. We became aware, however, that the most senior levels of management were not attending the programme.

We decided to adopt a different strategy in order to market the programme to senior managers. We introduced a second level of training, narrowing the target audience to middle and senior managers. We made the content more challenging, provided more structure for dealing with passive/aggressive behaviour and looked at individuals' rights and responsibilities at work. We have continued to run the standard programme for other staff.

I would say that the benefits to the organization of providing this type of training are reduced conflict and stress within the workforce and more confident staff able to make decisions more easily. Staff feel more able to make a more positive contribution to the areas they are involved in.

Case study

BBC Network Television

> **The Equal Opportunities Department, BBC Network Television (BBC TV), has made a commitment to equality of opportunity, and training is central to its equality drive. Assertiveness training is only a small part of the comprehensive range of courses offered to all staff with a particular focus on training for under-represented groups. All their training is funded by the equal opportunities budget so that as many people as possible have access to it.**

Carolann Ashton, Equality Training Manager

Our aim as a department is to implement a strategic equal opportunities programme to make BBC TV more representative of the people we serve, namely the viewers. We aim to do this in terms of workforce make-up and on-screen portrayal in the programmes we make. We have quantitative targets for the year 2000. They are:

- 50 per cent women (interim targets for 1996 are 30 per cent of senior management and 40 per cent of middle management)
- 8 per cent ethnic minority
- 3 per cent disabled people in the workforce

One way of reaching these targets is to make sure that staff have access to the most appropriate developmental training and that managers are also trained in managing diversity and recognize the positive benefits of training.

At present the BBC is undergoing a major upheaval and massive change in its culture and working practices, so it is important that training does not slip down the agenda. In some areas, getting staff released may become more of a problem as the workload has increased and the organization is down-sizing. Often if a course is needed, it is needed tomorrow and no one can give a guarantee of attendance a month down the line. However, in order for development training to succeed there must be a commitment from the organization, with the cost of investing in the potential of individuals being borne.

It is important for us to keep our training relevant and specific so that we can meet both individual and organizational needs. As the prime objective of a media organization is to create programmes and work to tight and pressing deadlines we have to tailor training events to this by remaining flexible. We must also advertise our courses frequently and as widely as possible so that they are not overlooked as a resource in this fast-moving climate. Providing a consultancy service and tailoring courses to departmental needs has been a major success.

We have developed assertiveness modules tailored to the specific needs of the following staff groups:

- women
- ethnic minorities
- disabled people
- lesbian and gay people
- all staff

We have split the training in this way to meet the unique and different needs of the groups involved. This decision was based on the needs of the organization, as expressed by the Directorate Implementation Group, which is made up of senior management, managers from pro-gramme, resource and support areas and includes controllers for BBC1 and BBC2, heads of departments, producers, trades union officials and staff who represent special interest groups (with whom we have regular contact), e.g. black workers group, disabled workers group, lesbian and gay group, working parents network, etc.

We also offer assertiveness as a core module to all staff. This is a com-munication organization; success is largely based on the way you inter-act with people and establish rapport. As such, developing skills in listening, being heard and dealing with difficult situations and people is essential.

However, we wanted to be certain that we were taking differences into account; for example, the way a disabled person deals assertively with a situation may not be the same as the way a non-disabled person would deal with the same situation. Equally, people from different cultures have different but equally valuable norms of interaction and behaviour. So our aim was not to clone all our staff to behave in a particular BBC way, but to explore the rich pattern of diversity and emphasize that as each individual is unique and they will have varying ways of behaving and of responding to situations.

It was also essential to get the right type of people to run the courses. We looked for skilled trainers with an inside and thorough knowledge of the issues of each particular group. So after selecting the best trainers, we now have a black woman delivering the assertiveness training for black staff and a disabled trainer delivering the courses for disabled staff, etc. As these are more specialized trainers it proved necessary to look outside the organization, although the majority of other courses are run in-house. It was also important to dispel stereotypes, so when the opportunity arose to employ a trainer, who incidentally happened to be disabled, to run the assertiveness course for women, we were delighted. She has proved to be excellent and a very positive role model.

The objectives of the assertiveness training are for staff to:

- develop their personal effectiveness given the realistic backdrop of the BBC culture
- discuss the often hidden reasons for their lack of career progression
- recognize their own power within the organization
- practise being assertive in a work situation
- develop a great sense of self-confidence when dealing with difficult situations
- develop strategies for dealing more effectively with harassment

All staff attending the assertiveness course fill in a pre-course questionnaire highlighting their needs. We ask:

- what are your objectives for the course?
- how is the current climate in the BBC affecting your career?
- what are the relevant issues for you as a black person/woman/ disabled person/lesbian or gay person/employee in this organization?
- how do you see your career progressing/developing in the BBC?
- what skills do you already possess to help you along this path?

This information helps us with the longer-term evaluation. As yet there have been no long-term evaluation studies because the assertiveness courses are relatively new and have not been running long enough. However, we anticipate 6-monthly and 12-monthly evaluations using a questionnaire and a sample of follow-up interviews with delegates and their managers. Of course, the most visible organizational evaluation would be a change in the workforce statistics to better reflect all staff at all levels.

It is also worth noting that the assertiveness courses are not offered in isolation, they are supported by a three-day developmental workshop for women, disabled and ethnic minority staff. These courses are for staff in non-management grades to further explore the issues of career development and look at ways of breaking down the barriers to a career in the BBC. These two courses are offered in tandem and are complementary. The assertiveness module is a practical day of skills and techniques, whereas the development courses are equally practical but allow time to reflect and discuss career development. They can be attended in either order because their content and ethos overlap, and they are run by the same person. The courses are also supported by a comprehensive equal opportunities policy implementation which means that heads of departments have quality and equality objectives written into their objectives and each department has its own departmental equality plan and equality staff group to take practical grass roots action. This is in conjunction with a well-developed harassment at work policy which includes helpline and counselling services.

Case study

Newry Volunteer Bureau

> **Working with volunteers mainly drawn from the unemployed presents a special challenge to the Newry Volunteer Bureau. One means of taking up the challenge has been to include assertiveness training as an integral part of volunteer training.**

Deborah Ui Dhaibhéid,
Training Officer

The Volunteer Bureau is an organization which provides people between the ages of 18 and 65 with placements within the caring sector. At present we have 400 volunteers registered with the bureau within 120 different projects and organizations.

The majority of our volunteers fall into the 25 + category, and about 70 per cent of this section of the volunteers' population are women. The geographical area in which our bureau operates is Newry and Mourne, an area of 40 miles' radius covering Newry Town, South Armagh and South Down. This area has the second highest rate of unemployment within the north of Ireland. It is not surprising, therefore, that many of our volunteers are people who want an alternative to unemployment, i.e. to give themselves something worth while to do with their time, as well as gaining valuable work experience within the caring field. In spite of the fact that Newry and Mourne is an area in need of substantial economic development, last year 46 per cent of our volunteers who were actively seeking work did move into employment, which is most encouraging.

For women registering with the bureau, engaging in voluntary work is often the first step they take on the road to rejoining the labour market.

Many of our women volunteers are people who have worked in some type of career since leaving school, have given up work to get married and rear families and who often come to us because their family commitments have been reduced (children at school, for example) and they want to take up voluntary work because it offers a safe environment and is flexible in that it can fit into the times when women are available.

In our experience of interviewing and placing women and trying to ascertain their needs, we often come across the 'I'm just a housewife' syndrome. Confidence levels and self-esteem are frequently low and it is for these reasons that we offer preparatory training for women. Assertiveness training is the main type of preparatory training offered. Once women have completed preparatory pre-vocational training, they can participate in other training areas.

The main areas of training on offer to volunteers in general are:

- **Direct on-the-job training in an area of care** For example, working with children, young people, physically disabled, people with learning difficulties, minority groups such as travellers, offering respite to carers, environmental schemes, charity shop work.
- **Skills training** Skills training is designed to complement and consolidate the skills acquired through work. We strive to provide training which is validated by the main awarding bodies, e.g. City & Guilds, BTec, RSA, short courses organized by the two universities in the north of Ireland.

An excellent example of the value of preparatory training for women can be found in the bureau's experience with a local mothers and toddlers group in Drumalane, a large housing estate in Newry town. The women from the group were very interested in the work of the bureau but they did not feel they could engage in voluntary work themselves. Approximately 5 years ago a partnership was made between the Volunteer Bureau and the Adult Education Department of the local Further Education College. The tutor at that time was Marie McStay, who was still working in adult education. She worked on an intensive personal development and assertiveness training package with the Drumalane women. After the first year at least six women came forward to do voluntary work. They became involved in providing literacy tuition to other volunteers who have learning difficulties. Others established a social club for the older people living in their immediate community. Three of the women are solely responsible for the organizing of the club, i.e. fund raising, planning a programme of activities, organizing outings, etc. Three other women have helped to revitalize the youth club in the area and are now active committee members. Some of the women have returned to education to take GCSEs and RSA Stage 1 and 2 in wordprocessing. One woman is currently in her second year of an HND course in Business and Finance at the

University of Ulster. Another woman is currently doing RSA Business Administration level 2.

All the women feel that the preparatory training they gained through their work with the trainer, Marie McStay, has allowed them to develop to their current level. The mothers and toddlers group still meets on a regular basis and, through the University of Ulster, the tutor works with the women to continue their adult education programme. The Volunteer Bureau has placed a volunteer child care worker to supervise the creche to allow the women to avail of the training.

In all, the Volunteer Bureau has benefited from the work of these volunteers, their local community has benefited from the women involving themselves in community development, and ultimately the women themselves have derived great personal satisfaction from a new-found way of valuing themselves, acknowledging their own capabilities and taking control of their lives and attempting to effect change in their own communities.

In conclusion therefore, we intend to continue our pre-vocational training for our volunteers. The Volunteer Bureau has always been accessible to people who initially felt themselves outside the confines of mainstream vocational training agencies and courses. We believe that assertiveness training is very valuable to our female volunteers as it acts as the springboard for them to look towards their own needs and consider their own career requirements.

Summary

This chapter has identified the main needs that assertiveness, if well taught and applied, will meet. These needs arise out of the changes in society, organizations and their relationship to the outside world, management styles, one-to-one communications, and the trend of moving from training to development. There are clear benefits of assertiveness to organizations, individuals and to trainers. The trainer's own use of assertiveness will be dealt with in more detail in the next chapter and the need for specific courses on assertiveness in Chapter 6. There also follow some case studies of organizations, their need for assertiveness and what they have done to satisfy the need.

References

Barham, K. and Rassam, C. (1989) *Shaping the Corporate Future*, Unwin Hyman, London.

Clark, N. (1991) *Managing Personal Learning and Change*, McGraw-Hill, Maidenhead.

Employment Gazette (1991) 'Labour force trends: the next decade', *Employment Gazette*, May.

Hammond, V. and Holton, V. (1991) *A Balanced Workforce? Achieving cultural change for women: a comparative study*, Ashridge Management Research Group, Berkhamsted, Herts.

Handy, C. (1985) *The Future of Work*, Basil Blackwell, Oxford.

Handy, C. (1990) *Inside Organisations*, BBC Books, London.

Handy, C. (1994) *The Empty Raincoat*, Hutchinson, London.

Harvey-Jones, J. (1988) *Making it Happen*, Fontana/Collins, London.

Kouzes, J.M. and Posner, B.Z. (1987) *The Leadership Challenge*, Jossey Bass, San Francisco.

Ross, R. and Schneider, R. (1992) *From Equality to Diversity*, Pitman, London.

Ryan, M. (1986) *Power and Influence in Organisations*, Manpower Services Commission, Sheffield.

Womack, J.P., Jones, D.T. and Roos, D. (1990) *The Machine that Changed the World*, Macmillan, Basingstoke.

4 The assertive trainer

In the previous chapter, we outlined some of the overall changes happening in society and in organizations which demand a different and changing response from training and development departments and strategies. In turn, this places a changed and changing demand on individual trainers themselves. The global views, intellectual crystal ball gazing, and mission statements are all very well, but how does all this translate into our day-to-day lives as trainers? The relevance and importance of assertiveness as a key skill in the trainer's tool box has already been covered. This chapter outlines the ways in which using assertiveness affects trainers both professionally and personally, including:

- your objectives
- the benefits
- the criteria
- self-assessment questionnaire
- hurdles to be overcome
- the assertive trainer's role
- assumptions

The chapter concludes with six case studies of trainers in different environments who describe the effect of using assertiveness on their personal and professional lives.

Your objectives

What do you want to achieve by using assertiveness? If you're new to training you may feel you already have enough to cope with, or may want to develop a skill with many applications. If you're an experienced trainer, you may feel excited or resentful at the idea of adding a new skill to your repertoire.

Here are some reasons other trainers have had for learning assertiveness:

'I want to be able to deal with aggressive participants without using the sarcastic clip which I'm so good at!'
'For my own self-esteem, I want to be better able to practise what I preach'
'I want to be able to cope with interruptions without getting so rattled'
'I want to be able to go home after working with a difficult group

without feeling torn apart'

'I want to be able to build a better rapport with my groups'

'I do a lot of skills training which is on the margins of assertiveness—I want to be able to incorporate it'

'I've done a lot of technical training and I want to move into communications skills. I understand the theory, but I feel vulnerable with the impromptu remarks'

Think about your own objectives for learning more about assertiveness. Be specific.

The benefits

Along with most other people, we've had struggles in learning and applying assertiveness. We believe it is a valuable skill in any form of training because:

- it gives a process for dealing with any situation
- it enables you to deal with situations with dignity
- it 'equals' the relationship between trainer and participant
- it increases effective communication
- it crosses barriers
- it ensures you treat your course participants with respect
- it gains you respect
- it reduces stress
- it diffuses aggression
- it enables you to recognize passive and aggressive behaviour and to work with them positively
- it enhances learning as disputes are dealt with
- it's less tiring and emotional in the long term
- it enables you to give and receive feedback constructively
- it reduces the chances of misunderstandings
- it enables you to be clear about your own views and needs when dealing with administrators, colleagues, clients and senior management
- it can be part of your own personal development
- it enables you to express your feelings constructively

In addition, when you are running an assertiveness course:

- it enables you to be a positive role model
- it increases your effectiveness and credibility
- it enhances the participants' learning

When running 'Training Trainer' courses, we encourage participants to think of as many difficult scenarios which they have come across, or might come across, in training. The point of this is to develop positive strategies to overcome these difficulties in the safety of the training room. At the end of a five-day course there will be up to 50 scenarios to be resolved. Over the years we've noted that the solution to 75–80 per cent of these scenarios can be summarized in one word—assertiveness.

Trainers' effectiveness can be diminished by their:

- lack of understanding of assertiveness as a useful tool on any course
- lack of experience in its use
- perceived fear of assertiveness diluting their formal authority in the training room

The criteria

What makes an assertive trainer? At the absolute minimum, someone who practises assertiveness in the training room, but for credibility, someone who applies assertiveness to all aspects of their professional life and, for preference, someone who applies assertiveness to all aspects of their life.

Assertive trainers:

- are aware of their own abilities and vulnerabilities
- are committed to the concept of assertiveness
- are striving to practise assertiveness in both personal and professional life
- haven't necessarily got it right yet
- are prepared to discuss their own successes and failures with assertiveness
- are open to feedback on their own behaviour
- are open to the possibilities of change and development for themselves

External or internal trainer?

You may be reading this book as an internal or freelance trainer. Alternatively you may be in a position to 'buy in' training staff on a regular or one-off basis, and the influences on your decision will often be more about budgets, availability, internal politics, and specialist skills, rather than the individual trainer's assertiveness skills. However, to help trainers use their own assertiveness, there are arguments for and against both categories of trainer.

The external trainer

Advantages:

- is not involved in internal politics so is more able to be open and assertive to people at all levels
- is not so influenced by past incidents and internal jealousies or alliances
- has 'novelty value', if people are unused to assertive behaviour
- is used to building effective 'instant' relationships

Disadvantages:

- assertiveness may not be a valued way of behaving in the organization and the trainer may be unaware of this
- external trainer may be desperate for repeat business and so not challenge key decision-makers
- does not always have to cope with the repercussions of the training

so it can be easier to let things go unchallenged (passive behaviour) or attempt to impose opinions (aggressive behaviour)

The internal trainer Advantages:

- may know the participants' situations and is therefore better able to understand and to suggest relevant action
- may know the internal politics and is therefore able to be more sensitive to issues which the participants may raise
- has to live with the repercussions of the training and so may have a greater interest in building positive relationships internally

Disadvantages:

- may find it difficult to deal assertively with participants who are senior to themselves
- may inadvertently intimidate participants who are junior to themselves
- may have to take assertive action to overcome the two previous
- may be seeking promotion or may fear redundancy or disapproval and so not express themselves assertively

Self-assessment questionnaire

Trainers are faced with challenges to their assertiveness every time they set up and run courses. Before going any further, complete the simple questionnaire (Figure 4.1) to give a temperature check of your own assertiveness.

Tick the a, b, c, or d response to identify how you tend to behave in these situations. Complete the questionnaire quickly. Your first intuitive responses are likely to be the best and most accurate.

When a colleague borrows your overhead projector pens regularly and forgets to return them to you, do you:

   (a)   drop hints at regular intervals   ☐
   (b)   buy some replacements   ☐
   (c)   explain the effect this has on you and ask for them back   ☐
   (d)   demand them back   ☐

A participant asks a question that seems sexist to you—do you:

   (a)   make a joke about it   ☐
   (b)   answer as best you can
   (c)   express some concern about the question and answer only if you feel OK about it   ☐
   (d)   point out the participant's sexism   ☐

Figure 4.1 Self-assessment questionnaire

**Your co-trainer publicly contradicts one of your favourite points.
Do you:**

(a)   get your own back later ☐

(b)   ignore it but feel put down ☐

(c)   tell the other trainer in private how annoyed you are
and ask them to stop contradicting you ☐

(d)   give the other trainer a piece of your mind for their
rudeness ☐

When someone criticizes your appearance do you:

(a)   say something like 'Well it's my most expensive
outfit/best suit' ☐

(b)   blush and say nothing ☐

(c)   check what is specifically being said and judge for
yourself ☐

(d)   tell him/her it's none of his/her business ☐

**A participant is late for the third time today. You have already
started. Do you:**

(a)   quip that you've managed OK without him/her ☐

(b)   just ignore them and feel insulted ☐

(c)   find out privately the reasons why and express your
feelings ☐

(d)   complain openly that it's the third time today and
insist that they've got to be punctual ☐

**Your participants don't seem to be listening when you try telling
them your views on the exercise they've just done. Do you:**

(a)   say something like 'Well if anyone's at all interested,
I'm ...' ☐

(b)   keep quiet ☐

(c)   say how you feel and that it's important to you to
tell them your views ☐

(d)   talk more loudly ☐

When you keep quiet in a situation is it because:

(a)   you know the silence will have an effect ☐

(b)   you are too upset or frightened to speak ☐

(c)   you have nothing to say ☐

(d)   you're sulking ☐

When you feel angry or upset with participants do you:

(a)   let one or two participants know over the tea break ☐

(b)   keep quiet ☐

(c)   try to say specifically how you feel ☐

(d)   explode ☐

Figure 4.1 (continued)

Your client or sponsor believes that all managers in a particular grade should be forced to attend a particular course. You think they should be self-nominating because it requires a high degree of personal commitment. Do you:

    (a) imply that it's not appropriate   ☐
    (b) go along with your client's/sponsor's view   ☐
    (c) explain your reasons for self-nomination and try to find a way that meets your and your client's need   ☐
    (d) dig your heels in and forcibly insist   ☐

You are due for a coffee break and the coffee hasn't arrived. Do you:

    (a) ring the caterers and ask 'What do you have to do to get a cup of coffee around here?'   ☐
    (b) carry on training till it arrives   ☐
    (c) phone and find out when it will be delivered and impress on them your displeasure and be clear about how quickly you want the coffee   ☐
    (d) get angry with the participants or the caterers because this has happened many times before.   ☐

Figure 4.1 (continued)

Then count up how many a's, b's, c's, and d's you've scored.

- Mostly b's—your behaviour tends to be passive
- Mostly c's—this shows that you tend to be assertive, but check that you actually do the things you say you do. Sometimes it is easy to see what the best solution is on paper, but a more passive or more aggressive response may slip out in the heat of the moment.
- Mostly a's and d's—your behaviour tends to be aggressive. The d's are directly aggressive, whilst the a's are indirectly aggressive and manipulative. Most people confuse assertive behaviour with aggressive behaviour, so it's not unusual to have a high score here.

The hurdles

Having looked at your current level of assertiveness, consider the hurdles in your path. They may be clearly defined or a complex mixture of several factors. The most usual difficulties are:

- not knowing about assertiveness
- your own childhood conditioning
- your relationship with yourself
- the responses from others when you've tried assertiveness
- 'notches' from the past
- not feeling assertive
- a difficult group
- not having had enough practice

Not knowing about assertiveness

Maybe that is why you're reading this book. Knowing the theory is a step in the right direction, but really understanding the concepts behind it is essential to be able to take action in the heat of the moment.

Be aware that there are many different approaches to assertiveness—you may want to read around the subject before trying again.

Your own childhood conditioning

Refer back to the section on 'head tapes' in Chapter 2 and consider which of your own head tapes are assertive, aggressive or passive. Some of these may not matter much in general conversation but have a great impact on your attempts to be assertive when training under pressure.

Your relationship with yourself

Up to now, you've explored your ability to be assertive with other people, but you also need to be aware of your ability to be assertive with yourself. This is manifest in the voices inside which can dramatically affect the outcome of events—'self-fulfilling prophecies'. These inner voices can also be aggressive, passive or assertive and can have a devastating effect on self-esteem.

For example: you are about to run a new one-day course on an unfamiliar subject. You've just discovered that the group are senior, highly educated and articulate, and that the quality of your workshop will determine the direction of further training in this area.

The conversation with yourself might go like this:

- **Passive voice**: 'It's not going to work. I'm not up to it. They're always setting me up for things like this. I'll drop a few hints and with a bit of luck someone else will do it. If the worst comes to the worst, I'll call in sick.'
- **Aggressive voice**: 'Right, I've got it all figured out and as the trainer, I know best. As long as they do as I say, it'll go fine. If it goes wrong, it won't be my fault.'
- **Assertive voice**: 'This is going to be a bit of a stretch for me but I know I'm good at my job. If difficulties crop up which I haven't foreseen, I'll go back to the ground rules and the basic ingredients.'

Your passive voice tells you:

- your views don't matter
- everyone else is better or more important
- you can't do it
- it's your fault
- your feelings are irrelevant
- you're not important
- there's every chance you'll fail

Your aggressive voice tells you:

- you've got it right

- alternative opinions are wrong
- it's somebody else's fault
- others should realize how good you are
- you'll do it brilliantly—as long as you can do it your way

Your assertive voice tells you:

- your opinion is valid
- alternative opinions are also valid
- what your feelings are
- you are able to express your feelings
- you can work with people to an outcome you feel happy with
- you are able to assess your own success and failure realistically
- your failures do not mean *you* are a failure
- you have previous life and work experience which you can draw upon

Think about the messages which you're sending yourself. Consider whether they change from work to when you're at home, and vice versa. Some people are aggressive at work and passive at home. Some people find it easier to be assertive with friends but have great difficulties with colleagues. What are your own tendencies?

Responses from others when you've tried assertiveness

Some people learn a little about assertiveness, but can hit problems if when they start putting it into practice they gain a negative or aggressive response. Although, intellectually, you may understand that this response is a result of fear, it may not stop the response hurting.

For example: Having attempted, for the first time, an assertive conversation with a colleague, you may be met with the directly aggressive:

- derisive laughter
- 'Is that it then? Is that assertiveness?'
- 'Are you doing it now then?'
- 'XXXX off!'
- 'Hey—listen to this everyone!'
- 'Don't you start that assertiveness rubbish on me!'
- 'Just leave the assertiveness stuff in the course room will you?'

Or the indirectly aggressive:

- being polite to your face and then laughing about you behind your back

Or the passive:

- complying with your request, but internally resenting it and building the notches for an explosion in two months' time.

Have any of these happened to you? Starting to build your own assertiveness when the people around you are not used to it can be a difficult stage.

Unfortunately it's also when you have the least experience. The answer is to take it in small steps, to discard assertiveness when you don't want to cope with the consequences, not to be hard on yourself if it doesn't go well, and keep trying!

Your expectations of others can also become self-fulfilling prophecies, so also remain open minded, because it's more likely that your attempt at assertiveness will encourage a positive or even an assertive response.

'Notches' from the past

It's especially difficult to behave assertively with someone with whom there are a lot of unresolved difficulties from the past. It takes a great deal of courage to deal assertively with these notches.

You may also have locked yourself into a pattern of aggressive or passive behaviour with this person which is almost impossible to break, and although you can behave assertively with most other people, you're reduced to an aggressive monster or a passive wreck with this one particular individual or group.

Is there such a person(s) for you? If so, have an assertive conversation with yourself to acknowledge your feelings about it and to set yourself up for assertiveness success next time. You may even initiate the conversation to prevent it assuming even greater significance.

For example: a trainer whose behaviour is usually impeccably assertive is always thrown when confronted with outrageous sexism from a particular manager. Although she understands, intellectually, the assertive response, her fear that the strength of her feelings will overwhelm her results in a habitual passive response. She just backs off. Each time this happens she feels she has let herself and others down, adding to the strength of her anger and hurt and therefore making it even more difficult for her next time.

Not feeling assertive

You don't have to be feeling assertive to behave assertively, although this leads us into an assertive circle because by expressing that you're not feeling assertive, you could be behaving assertively! This category acknowledges that most of us don't feel especially assertive sometimes and so there will be occasions when we give in to the temptation to take a participant down a peg or two, or when we accept an offensive remark passively. As outlined in Chapter 2, behaving assertively also means making choices, so part of assertiveness involves making an active choice to also behave aggressively or passively. Use assertiveness when you want to. It's up to you to decide the criteria for your own assertiveness, so some level of self-awareness and honesty with yourself is needed.

A group or person whose behaviour you experience as difficult

Behaving assertively in training when people are committed, interested and responding positively is easier than when you experience people as difficult, or worse, feel you're battling for your survival!

In terms of assertiveness, all forms of behaviour make different demands on the trainer. This is where assertiveness can become a real lifeline, ensuring that you and the group or person come out of the situation with your self-respect and integrity intact. More on this later in the chapter.

Not having had enough practice

The solution to this is to keep at it! However, don't set yourself up to fail by attempting to be assertive everywhere and all the time. Decide for yourself how you want to build up your experience. Many people decide to leave the really frightening situations alone and to build up their assertiveness experience on smaller situations where the outcome isn't very important to them. Other people approach it from the opposite direction, using assertiveness in the big situations where the outcome is very important to them. Some people keep assertiveness for dealing with specific situations or individuals, whilst others try to integrate it into all their relationships with the objective of it becoming a regular habit.

The assertive trainer's role

The trainer's use of assertiveness and its influence on the trainer's role will obviously be influenced by the objectives and type of training. A health and safety course with specific procedures which must be obeyed may have less scope for discussion and less flexibility in the behaviours required than, say, a course on running meetings or a career development course.

However, the assertive trainer has a wider range of styles and behaviours available and is therefore more able to accommodate effectively the individual participants.

Figure 4.2 shows a spectrum of behaviour open to trainers. You may want to add others of your own to the blank spaces at the bottom of the list.

There are occasions when working at the extreme ends of a spectrum is totally appropriate, but the assertive trainer will mostly be operating within the broad shaded area in the centre, whilst still able to move swiftly across when required.

This means that the assertive trainer's role is defined as follows:

What it is	What it isn't
a coach	a counsellor
positive	authoritarian
honest	cynical
in control	sarcastic
supporting	negative
challenging	providing magic answers
emphasizing	timid
confident	waffly
informal	an ego trip
open	patronizing
clear	prescriptive
dignified	judgmental
equal	superior
approachable	point-scoring
flexible	in a hurry
organized	therapist
disciplined	prejudiced
informing	putting down
encouraging independence	sympathetic
balanced	encouraging dependence
	imposing
	manipulative
	dismissive

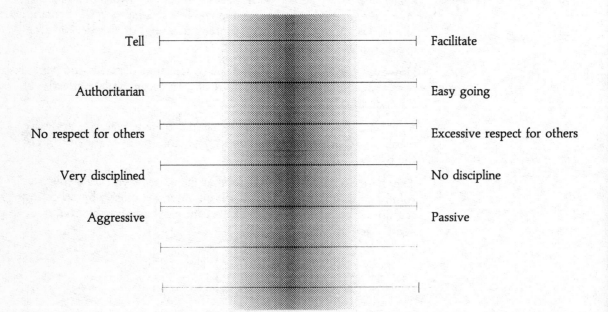

Figure 4.2 *Spectrum of behaviour*

It is especially important to remember your limitations, as trainers may be tempted to encourage participants to raise complex or sensitive personal difficulties as raw material for practice. Trainers are not counsellors or therapists, and there is danger that a participant may be encouraged to raise an issue which the trainer does not have the time, skill or experience to deal with.

Mairi Macleod is aware of this danger in her case study, whilst Stella Wiseman, in her case study at the end of Chapter 6, urges caution:

Issues such as dealing with self-criticism, or combating a negative self-image which may stem from childhood experiences, can rarely be solved in a few hours within a group of people who hardly know each other. Assertiveness training should not take the place of counselling.

As part of the trainer's preparation (not just for assertiveness courses), have contact details with you of professionals who can help, in case someone with a real difficulty is on your course, and be clear with the participant about what are realistic expectations of you and the course.

Alternatively, if, in addition to being a trainer, you are also a qualified counsellor or therapist, you may be able to help participants in difficulty in that capacity. In which case, be very clear with them about your different roles and enter into a counselling or therapy relationship with them only at their request, and totally separately from the course.

Assumptions

The definition of assertiveness emphasizes the importance of self-respect, and respect for others. One of the areas where lack of respect for other people can be displayed is through the assumptions made about them. There are particular difficulties for trainers in this respect. The easier assumptions to deal with are the ones of which you're aware, but you may also have blind spots. Here is a list of some assumptions which trainers sometimes make and which negate the concept of respect for others. The assumptions given are not in any particular order, and relate to a wide range of different types of courses. See if any of yours are here, and add any of your own or your colleagues that you wish to be more aware of.

Assuming that participant(s):

- want to change
- are looking for development
- are looking forward to the course
- are pleased to be on it
- want to be assertive
- want support
- want this course
- have a difficulty to overcome
- want to talk about personal issues

- have had a strong role model, e.g. mother or boss
- have or had parents
- want to share opinions, knowledge
- will understand first time what is said
- have reading skills
- have a garden/spare room/TV
- have a car/telephone/video
- accept your philosophy
- have children or want them
- are honest
- remember Suez, John F. Kennedy's assassination or any other specific event in history!
- speak the same language
- do things by choice, not duty or pressure
- can talk about taboo subjects
- understand issues
- will talk more about things if encouraged
- have partners
- want partners
- have a partner of the opposite sex
- have partners who are supportive/not supportive
- like to be called 'dear', 'sweetheart', 'ladies', 'girls', 'chaps', 'boys', etc.
- will question you when they don't understand
- will say what they mean
- know what you think they know
- will understand jargon
- are pleased to be living where they are
- were born here/not born here
- understand the culture of the organization or country
- have personal relationships
- are married
- have had particular life experiences
- are young, and therefore not experienced
- have money
- are glad to be a women/man
- take holidays
- drink alcohol
- know current or past TV programmes, pop stars, music, films, etc.
- have the same sense of humour as you
- have a social life/friends/family
- want a social life/friends/family
- were brought up with their natural parents
- are interested in sex/have a sex life
- disabilities are visible

Add your own:

The assertive trainer strives to minimize making assumptions and works on the basis that everyone:

- has their own thoughts, opinions, ideas, credos, philosophies and beliefs
- has their own feelings, and that the feelings that one individual may experience in relation to an incident may be substantially different to the feelings of any other member of the group. Feelings relate to the previous experiences and events in a person's life
- has the right to equal respect as a human being. People may have different skills, qualities, and experiences and all have valid but perhaps very different contributions to make.

Case studies

In the case studies which follow, trainers from a variety of backgrounds explain their experience of assertiveness, and how assertiveness has affected them and their approach to training. The case studies are all written in the trainer's own words with an introductory paragraph added by us.

Case study

> **Jane describes the curiosity which first drew her to find out about assertiveness, her initial scepticism and her own introduction to it. She gives examples of her present use of assertiveness on both assertiveness and other forms of training.**

Jane Beck,
Beck Associates

My first encounter with assertiveness training was a marvellous revelation, and offered a tantalizing glimpse of the possibility of smooth communications between individuals both at work and in personal life. For someone like me who had been brought up by parents for whom the words 'trouble and strife' might have been invented; who had worked in the hospitality industry, when artistic temperament combines with constant pressure to produce situations when tools are laid down and tears frequently shed; who had on many occasions struggled and failed, to control her own temper; this was a revelation indeed. I just knew I had to find out some more!

Eleven years ago, as one of a group of consultants who were specializing in training initiatives for women, I was invited by the (then) Manpower Services Commission to take part in a one day programme on assertiveness training. The programme was run by Myrtle Berman, a pint-sized but power-packed consultant who has since become a respected friend. She was one of the first consultants in the UK to run these programmes, and her programme made a deep and lasting impression for both the content and delivery. I subsequently invited her to run a series of programmes for women managers in the hospitality industry;

they were also impressed. In my subsequent dealings with those managers I saw aggression become softer and the more passive women become bolder. Here was proof positive that this was one training technique that really worked.

One of my strongest memories of my own initiation into the technique is of being asked to stand up and state my positive strengths—for one minute only. I leapt to my feet, keen to get it over with, and although the minute seemed like infinity, I kept talking to the end. I was followed by a sharply dressed man for whom the word 'charisma' was something of an understatement. His voice flowed like warm, brown treacle as he told us all what a great guy he was. After 30 seconds he dried up completely, whereupon my own self-esteem soared! I knew then that I had to become an assertiveness trainer.

I worked with Myrtle on nine separate courses and took copious notes and listened avidly as she dealt with questions and coached delegates in role play techniques. I read Anne Dickson and Ken and Kate Back and, through my involvement with management training for women at the Civil Service College, I discovered the effects that passive, aggressive and assertive managers have on their staff. I learned the use of assertive behaviour in solving problems. After a four-year initiation period, I began to run my own programmes.

My own courses are usually two-day events. I have now run them for women only, men only and women and men together. It was something of a revelation to me to discover that men too find it difficult to be assertive.

I find it useful to run a one-day follow-up programme six months after the initial workshop. Delegates can then share their successes and problems and together we can work out strategies for dealing with the latter.

Working as a woman in a world where most of the power is held by men, it is all too easy to develop an aggressive behavioural style. I believe I was no exception to this rule before I began to practice assertive techniques. I now listen attentively using appropriate eye contact and body language, and assertiveness has also helped my negotiating skills.

When I am running courses I always ask delegates to pay each other compliments. The recipient has to listen and repeat the compliments back. It's amazing how many people turn off the moment that someone says something nice to them, and I frequently have to ask the donor to repeat the message for a second time. Assertiveness can be a real confidence-booster and a tremendous aid to restoring self-esteem. For example, a man will be badly shaken if his wife has walked out in favour of someone else. The scars are usually quite visible. A woman may still be hearing the head tapes engendered by verbal abuse from either parent, when her only option was to grin and bear it. These are just two examples plucked at random from delegates to recent courses. Both provide a challenge for the trainer who, using the techniques, can help to restore in an individual a real sense of their own worth.

The techniques of assertion help enormously when I am running other courses. Assertiveness is a crucial factor in effective time management, in self-promotion and image building, in the control of stress. It is useful for the trainer to be able to deal with the demanding and dominating delegate; there's one on every course and they need careful handling to enable other course members to get a look in. Similarly a quieter, non-participating person can be brought out.

My own attitude before becoming a practitioner was initially one of curiosity, closely followed by scepticism. The desire to know more, coupled with the fear that this was 'just another nine day wonder'. I am happy to say that having satisfied the one and dispelled the other I am now able to write with absolute conviction that here is a technique that really works. It can be quickly learned and easily mastered given the desire to improve communications with friends and colleagues.

Case study

> **Christine describes the reactions of participants to learning assertiveness and how it has affected both her personal life and her work life. She also makes the important point that learning assertiveness is an ongoing process, requiring constant monitoring and practice.**

Christine Baines
Christine Baines
Consultancy

I had always thought I was an 'assertive woman' until I was actually 'trained' to deliver assertiveness training. I had never been on an assertiveness training course as I really believed I didn't need it! I now know, and tell all the women who come on my courses, that most women who believe they are assertive but have had no training, are in fact, politely aggressive.

Delivering training in assertiveness has really helped me with my own assertive behaviour and agenda, and I now firmly believe and practice assertiveness as a life style. I think assertiveness is much more than resolving conflict and believe that if one makes assertiveness part of one's behaviour pattern, there is far less conflict to resolve!

In my experience of training in the north of England, many women do not understand the difference between a thought and a feeling. This is the biggest barrier to assertive behaviour, which in addition to the oft-prevailing attitude that one should not consider what one feels to be remotely important, makes it hard for many women to accept that they can say no, or object to being 'put upon'. I still think that the area of self-esteem needs work, before assertive behaviour is completely assimilated. Most of the women who come through my courses get to grips with the theory of assertiveness, the ingredients and rules, but can still not identify (or are unwilling to admit it) and thus articulate how they feel. The continual reinforcement I make during courses has enabled me to articulate this effectively in my own life and areas of conflict.

Assertiveness is helpful when dealing with the one or two disruptive delegates one always gets on courses. It enables me to clearly say how I feel and think about the interruption or disruption, or the hijacking of other colleagues' 'space'. It is very effective also when asking groups to re-form and face front to say 'I actually feel foolish talking to your back; I think you are ignoring me.' They are usually horrified and re-form immediately.

I will add though, that there are still times when I walk round the block, or rehearse in the car, talking to myself ...

> 'Demonstrate understanding' ... how will you do that?
> 'Say what you think and feel' ... what do you think and feel?
> 'Say specifically what you want to happen' ... what do you want to happen?

so it's not all off pat yet!

Case study

> **Colin Russell is a very experienced trainer on BT's Management Development Programmes. As such he runs assertiveness courses for a wide range of staff, and also trains other trainers to deliver assertiveness events. In this case study he describes how assertiveness has been important to him in four areas:**
> - **his own behaviour**
> - **running management development events**
> - **running assertiveness events**
> - **when training and developing other trainers.**

Colin Russell,
BT

Assertiveness and myself   I moved into Management Development Programmes around six years ago, and after about two years was invited to attend an assertiveness event to develop my own skills and to help me move into trainer training. I have often said that the assertiveness event changed my life—probably having the biggest impact on me of any other training event that I had attended. The three key pillars for me in assertiveness are: the management of feelings, the management of my own self-esteem, and the recognition of the rights of both individuals or parties. It was the last that had the greatest impact on me; I had spent the majority of my life walking around with everybody else's rights on the shelf, whilst mine were tucked away in the cupboard, so one of the biggest impacts on me was to get my rights out of the cupboard and put them next to the rights of other people. I had to be very careful that the pendulum didn't suddenly swing from one extreme to the other, so I worked on balancing the rights of both myself and the people around me.

Together with the matter of feelings (an area which I have explored for myself at various levels), and the constant need to build up my own self-esteem, the recognition of rights gave me a tremendous amount of strength and courage and energy to start to communicate more assertively. When I came back from the event and in the months that followed, people (including my line manager) made comments to me that I was a much stronger individual, and less likely to bow in the wind. From the initial successes as a result of that event, the predominant one was a success on holiday, when I was given a damp and unclean caravan for an exorbitant amount of money. In the past, I'd have whinged and moaned about it during the holiday and for months afterwards. Instead, I assertively made a request to have the caravan changed, and felt really good standing in an almost brand new caravan 20 minutes or so later! That feeling of success gave me a tremendous impetus and from then on, a strong belief in the communication skills of assertiveness, and what it can do for me and the people around me.

Assertiveness in management development

As a result of using assertiveness, I've been a stronger person in the office, in teams, and in meeting new people, as it's given me a lot more confidence and courage, and enabled me to communicate my own thoughts and beliefs. Receiving criticism has never been much of a problem, but I've had to work on receiving praise positively. In terms of management development, being able to help individuals communicate better to others on courses, to return on time, to restrain their behaviour, and to give them criticism and praise clearly and honestly has helped my professionalism.

It's also helped me in terms of working with and developing relationships with co-trainers. I remember one particular occasion when my co-trainer made a number of remarks to participants, drawing attention to a small error I had made during a training session. This particular trainer and myself were very good friends. Afterwards I told him that I'd like him to refrain from making any more remarks about this simple error, in case participants actually believed that I was a fool, as my friend was indicating. He accepted the feedback, but it wasn't until the next day that he thanked me for the feedback that I'd given, and said that it was very important to him when he'd reflected on it on the way home. From that moment on, although we were friends initially, it brought us a lot closer together as friends and colleagues. So the importance of assertiveness in terms of building relationships, including relationships with co-trainers, has stood out for me.

In addition, we constantly work with senior managers, who also come in as guest speakers on courses. The need to be assertive with some of our senior management team is paramount and, again, success in this area has given me a lot of courage to continue to work on my assertiveness skills.

For example: a very senior manager in the company on a training event was obviously very busy, having worked on his telephone and fax in the car on the way to the event. He brushed my colleague and myself aside very brusquely, gave us very little eye contact, and communicated with us very abruptly and rudely. When he was introduced to the team he was going to be working with, he made the comment, referring to us: 'Oh, these are the guys that are on holiday.' After he made a second comment of this type, I was getting very angry and annoyed. After plucking up the courage and confidence to approach him, I spoke to him and said I didn't find it a joke, that I worked very hard on the event, and I would like him to refrain from further comments of this type. He immediately said it was his humour and apologized. From then on, he gave me a lot of eye contact, started to speak to me as a human being, and our relationship grew stronger throughout the event. We've met on a number of occasions since, and he still remembers that time, and again, it really has shown me the power of effective communication and how it brings people closer together, rather than forcing them apart. So assertiveness has helped me to develop myself within teams in training with participants, with co-trainers, and with senior manager guests.

BT's assertiveness event   Our assertiveness event is of three days duration, to which individuals bring their own issues. We include input sessions on self-esteem, management of feelings, and rights, followed by key steps to help in key behaviour areas and as many practice sessions as possible. This event had been running for about 18 months when we introduced an interactive video element as well (details in the Appendix). The importance of this is that, before the course, participants have the opportunity to get to grips with the knowledge on the interactive video and do some pre-course work. For example, they look at their own assertiveness skills, and (probably more importantly at this stage) observe other behaviours around them. They identify whether they prefer to behave assertively, indirectly aggressively, passively or aggressively. They look at the impact that that behaviour has on them, and on the people around them. This information is then brought to the training event along with real issues, and this really has helped people understand assertiveness a lot quicker and allowed us to use the course for building skills and confidence. The emphasis on practice in the three days gives them the opportunity to practise in safety, to feel what it is like to be communicated with assertively, to observe assertiveness in action and then to give constructive criticism and praise. Normal action planning takes place at the end of the course, but certainly the interactive video linked to workplace pre-work and the training course has made it a far more effective event.

An important area which we focus in on is the managing of 'put-downs' and sarcasm, and really challenging people on this. We're not looking to cut down on humour, but we do explore to what degree the sarcasm is really hurting the receiver; that what is often thought of as office banter always affects somebody at the bottom of the 'office league', and it's this individual who feels the hard edge.

Training trainers in assertiveness

For four years I've been involved in trainer training and trainer development. This is one of the few subjects on which we run trainer training events and that's because we recognize that whilst our trainers can pick up the content easily, we need to know to what degree they have taken on the philosophy of assertiveness, to what degree can they actually model assertiveness in terms of the language, the behaviour, and self-disclosures—also in terms of their using their own life examples, and to what degree they actually help other people get underneath the basic steps and to look at the philosophy and what it means to individuals. We may also need to challenge some of their thoughts and their beliefs and their current way of behaving to ensure that they are able to practise what they preach. Trainers come on a two and a half day training event where they practise delivering the key sessions from the assertiveness event. Our people come with a high level of training skills anyway, so the key areas that we work on are the modelling of assertiveness during the training event, that is making sure that they model assertive language, and do not put themselves down, etc. In addition to modelling assertiveness, we also look at the content and material that they're delivering, their ability to give and elicit good clear examples, and to self-disclose (again as a positive model) where appropriate, but to self-disclose to a degree that doesn't impair the participants' learning.

Prior to the actual running of the sessions each trainer has an opportunity in plenary to discuss their thoughts and feelings about assertiveness, and this is where they think about where they are with assertiveness and talk about their successes, and how they are developing this skill. One frequent statement is 'I haven't had the opportunity yet to practise the skill'. When this happens, we know we've got quite a bit of work to do, in helping this particular trainer understand that it is not something you switch in, switch on, and switch off. It is not a quick-fix trick that you pull out of the bag, it's a way of communication that you can take throughout your home and work life. At this point, I have to be careful about being 'evangelistic' about the skill and philosophy of assertiveness, but it is something that we have to work with and challenge quite hard on trainer training events if our trainers are going to really work with the philosophy of assertiveness rather than using it as a quick-fix list of tricks.

Following the trainer training event, trainers then run two events which are observed and supported by an experienced trainer. Here we aim to encourage them to get underneath the training material and key steps, and to really work with the needs of the individuals and the group. Trainers are encouraged to challenge, question and help participants explore any lack of enthusiasm or resistance.

Finally, what I look for in trainers is the ability to work in 'real time', that is encouraging participants to communicate assertively back, on any issue that's live at the time. **For example**: if a participant doesn't want to do a skill practice or feels really uncomfortable, the trainer needs to encourage the individual to find out what the problem is, and to help them to communicate that assertively, maybe by saying: 'I do not wish to do a skill practice'. Then the trainer needs to reflect back to the participant that what they've actually done is communicate very clearly and honestly their wish not to do a skill practice. In addition, they may have managed their feelings of anger, annoyance, and irritation, and they've communicated them. So it's important to demonstrate to participants the benefits and value of assertiveness in all situations, not just in the formal skill practice sessions.

In summary, the philosophy of assertiveness has had a very big impact on me. There is no question about where I would be in management development without this. It has helped me progress, and has given me a lot of success. It has also helped me in my management development career through helping me work with my colleagues, through working with participants, trainers and guest speakers. How we've developed the training event has been very beneficial, in actually getting people to experience, observe and develop assertiveness skills in the workplace.

Case study

> **Barbara's story illustrates the common misunderstanding about the differences between aggressive and assertive behaviour, her own—often uncomfortable—journey away from one towards the other, and her use of assertiveness in a range of training.**

Barbara Peel,
The Learning Curve

I have worked as a trainer for eight years; four years in the private sector, and four as a freelance trainer.

My entry into the trainer's role was from a management position in the recruitment industry. I was working at middle management level for an industrial and technical recruitment agency, whose directors and senior management were predominantly male. Because I had a good reputation for staff development and was perceived as having 'high standards' I was approached to be the training manager of the organization.

At this time I considered myself to be assertive, although I hadn't received any training or coaching in the subject. My management skills were gained by observation, some coaching, and trial and error. The culture of the organization was young, dynamic and what I now know to be aggressive! Constructive criticism was a little-used skill, and meetings often degenerated into personal critical comments, point-scoring, raised voices, and so on.

As I became more confident and skilled, I was promoted to a position where I was involved in recommending human resource strategies and policies. This often led to conflict and aggressive behaviour, from all sides, including me! I hated this way of working, but didn't seem to be able to escape from the spiral.

Very soon after leaving the company and setting up my own business in 1990, I realized how my behaviour had been affected and influenced by the culture I had experienced. I had adopted what is sometimes described as a 'male management style' with little or no room for more feminine approaches. I had been called 'bossy', 'strident', etc., yet at the same time praised for my results. What a mixed bag of messages! No wonder I was confused.

In late 1990, I came across the *Springboard Women's Development Workbook*, wrote to the authors, Liz Willis and Jenny Daisley, telling them how impressed I was with their efforts, and in July 1991 became an accredited trainer. By this time I had read more on assertiveness and realized that what I thought was assertive behaviour quite often was in fact aggressive. This made me look at all aspects of my life through new eyes, a process that was often very revealing and uncomfortable.

As I started to deliver Springboard workshops, it hit home just how important it was for me to continually evaluate my own behaviour, both at work and at home. Like a lot of other women, I initially had a reluctance to express my feelings. I was OK with saying what I wanted to happen, but actually saying things like, 'I feel angry' was very challenging.

I have a reputation with the people in my life of being strong, dependable, reliable and organized! So I allowed myself to be used, by several people in particular, as their 'Rock of Gibraltar'. As we know, it is a nice feeling to be needed and liked. The result of all this was a draining of my batteries, and often some feelings of resentment (minor). I now cope with these situations much better, usually by negotiating what I can offer, for how long and when. And surprise, surprise, they still like me!

My work involves me in other types of training, often with mixed-gender groups, and I have changed my approach to certain situations. For example, when someone is displaying anger I don't automatically assume it's directed at me personally, so I can be more objective in my handling of the situation. Or when, as is often the case, participants want my time for one-to-one during my lunch hour or after the 'official day' has ended, I don't just acquiesce and mumble to myself on the way home, as I used to, but deal with their requests assertively, sometimes by offering alternative arrangements or by suggesting other sources for what they need.

I particularly find assertiveness relevant when working on topics like communication and inter-personal skills. I do a lot of work on appraisal skills and giving staff ongoing feedback on their performance, areas where the techniques of assertiveness are invaluable.

When I recommend to a client that certain individuals would benefit from assertiveness training, the response is often negative—comments like 'They are bossy enough already', 'Don't change her, I like her the way she is' (from a director commenting on his passive secretary). Potential participants are often put off by the perceived militant 1970s theme of the training; the 'turning wimps into warriors' syndrome. I have also found a great reluctance from aggressive-style people to attend workshops, and this reaction has come from both genders.

I continue to review my own behaviour as honestly as I can, and accept that we all have good and bad days. On those days when I wish I hadn't got out from under the duvet, I certainly don't try to deal with my more difficult issues, but instead choose to be more passive. Over-all, I feel I have more confidence in my abilities as a trainer, and am better able to cope with most situations.

Case study

> **Nicky Stevenson's story shows how the assertive trainer is able to deal with any situation which crops up and the import-ance of being able to practise what you preach, especially when in the spotlight.**

Nicky Stevenson,
The Guild

I've been training as part of my work for about six years, initially aspects of business development, within the co-op sector, and gained a qualification—a City & Guilds 730 in 1989. I've never received training in assertiveness and for this reason never offered straight assertiveness courses. The only time I did was a disaster, because the person commis-sioning the training and I decided that the group she wanted me to work with needed assertiveness training, whereas the group itself had asked for presentation skills. Lesson 1—don't do assertiveness with people who want to do something else.

Having said that, we always did bits of assertiveness on longer courses aimed at, for example, people starting a business because when they go and meet their bank manager, these skills are extremely useful. This is where I have felt happiest using assertiveness, because people are often put off by the term but in this context they appreciate the practical implications.

I think lots of aspects of assertiveness are useful in other contexts, on other courses. Saying 'no', having a right to change one's mind, and having a right to make mistakes, are the aspects to which people particularly relate. I also think the last two are very useful to men, and that in general, using assertiveness in other contexts means that men get the opportunity to gain assertiveness skills in a context with which they feel comfortable, because no one will point the finger at them.

My own experience of using assertiveness is that it helps one boss people about without them minding! For example, getting the Women's Institute back from their tea breaks and quietening groups down prior to addressing them, etc.

The particular incident which springs to mind is when I was co-training on a general person development course, about two years ago. We were using a local music and arts centre as a venue, and were in one end of the main auditorium which was sectioned off for us. Just after doing the session on assertiveness, a band started tuning up next door, making us totally inaudible, so all eyes were on me with this sense of expectation as I went over to remonstrate with the sound technician.

He hadn't know we were there and there was nothing he would do about it anyway, because they had a gig that night. My natural inclination is to err on the aggressive side of assertiveness, but with all eyes upon me, I had to be seen to be impeccably assertive.

I agreed that it wasn't his fault, that there was clearly a problem with the booking system, and suggested that we go to the office and let them resolve the problem. When we got there, there was was some general shrugging and the repeat that there was a gig that night. So I asked whether anyone was in the second (smaller) auditorium upstairs, and as there wasn't said what I wanted to happen, which was that at no extra charge, we would be moved upstairs and that they, the office staff, would come immediately and move our tables, chairs and equipment, as the students had been inconvenienced enough already. At this suggestion, they all started running about with chairs and overhead projectors.

Within 10 minutes we were starting again and no one had lost their temper or been made to take the blame. The course participants were terribly impressed—as was my colleague, as indeed was I—that this was such an effective demonstration of assertiveness. I knew I'd done it because I couldn't very well do anything else under the circumstances, but it made me aware of how little energy and anxiety had been wasted, and how we'd all been able to carry on with what we were doing, with the minimum fuss.

Case study

> **With an education background, Mairi's story outlines her experience with assertiveness inside an organization and as a management skill. She also describes, in some detail, the way she runs assertiveness courses herself and the participants' responses.**

Mairi Macleod
Mairi Macleod
Associates

I turned to assertiveness for myself when I had my first management role. I carried a lot of head tapes about being good, caring, responsible, patient and understanding, but had no skills for handling conflict or addressing issues directly with people.

One example of this was when I set up an office for a whole team because I needed to improve their ability to work as a team. One man resisted, retaining his old desk in another building. In my head I understood why this might suit him; I patiently waited for him to want to join the team. In the meantime, I was swallowing some anger because it was sabotaging the work of the team. It never occurred to me to talk to him because 'good mothers always know what's best for their children and take the responsibility for making everything all right for everybody'.

Through *Cosmopolitan* magazine, I signed up for a day course with Anne Dickson on assertiveness training. She presented assertive behaviour with humour and skill. I then role-played the above work problem. Like a skilled surgeon, Anne cut through the head tapes that prevented my dealing with this. We established my right to make the request; clarified exactly what I wanted him to do; and checked out the words for saying this directly.

I went back to work, handled the situation successfully, and was a life-long convert to assertive ways of behaving. Anxious to spread the good news, I attended an accreditation course run by Anne Dickson. This was lengthy training of about 400 hours.

Before I turn to a description of delivering assertiveness training, I will describe how it became part of all the work I did in my organization. I was a faculty director in a college of further education with a cross-college responsibility for human resource development.

As well as being a more effective way of communicating with people it affected my design of many systems. Personal development interviews for staff were based on training in assertive communication. Compliance to equal opportunities policy was ensured through an assertive confrontation model. Equally, self-managed teams were trained in assertive communication behaviours. Although the returns were enormous there were some negatives. I was perceived as 'too powerful' in the organization. I was also perceived as less than human because I didn't engage in the blaming and rubbishing that goes on in organizations.

Senior male managers who endorsed these behaviours for curriculum management rejected them for 'real' management. One particular manager of the 'slash and burn' variety labelled it 'soft'. It needs to be articulated constantly that assertive human resource management is the 'hard' way to manage discipline, appraisal, redundancy. It is more effective than 'slash and burn'.

To turn now to delivering assertiveness programmes. I have run public courses; courses for public and private sector organizations; courses for international women at Durham University. I have run women-only and mixed courses. I run programmes in a very structured way; the content and skills building on what goes before. I find this works because clients can feel a safe structure while exploring something that may change their whole behaviour and have consequences for their life. It also ensures feelings of success. By tackling small manageable changes in competence, insight is gained to handle bigger changes.

I have a clear view of what constitutes a trainer as opposed to a therapist. Where a client arrives in a state which requires one-to-one counselling I will not continue training. I have a network of counsellors and complementary health practitioners whom I trust. I present this list to the client simply as information, emphasizing they must make the decision themselves.

The most important single thing I do is endorse people's right to their personal power. As a trainer, I have to be on guard against being handed their power. I use my expertise and authority to manage a safe process. Enabling that may include being 'bossy' about commitment and attendance. This will see people through stages of resistance. Life choices belong with the client. I don't need to be liked and if blaming the trainer is part of the process, I can handle that. I find it a very exciting moment when I feel a measurable shift from dependence on the trainer to self-reliance. When the client's life changes for the better, they tend to credit you with 'guru' qualities. It is really important not to own this. I always say out loud to them 'but you did it yourself', which is accurate and it reminds me to empower them.

In the United Kingdom, the cultural norms of politeness, sensitivity and Christianity make refusing requests the most difficult part of the course. I have run courses for volunteer youth and community workers who found the concept difficult because of the caring nature of their role. On the other hand, the part of the course dealing with handling criticism is well received. Having a skill to handle situations appears to be very liberating.

I teach people to manage the jokey behaviour of others when they know they are attending an assertiveness course. We find specific words to handle these situations. We also explore the fears of others confronted by a potential shift of power. There are still people who prefer to lie 'I just tell him I am cake decorating—he's not interested anyway'.

Working with an international group requires in addition an understanding of intercultural communication. A discussion of this can be found in works on human communication. As a lecturer in communication I was fortunate to have this background. A course with an international group needs more time at each exploratory phase of the process in order to match perceptions and discuss cultural norms, value systems and beliefs. Given that, a process in which clients manage their own learning using their own life experience and progressing at their own pace transcends national boundaries.

I am indebted to Anne Dickson for managing an excellent training process for me, for her clear analyses, for modelling assertive behaviour, and for her generosity in freeing the Redwood network to manage themselves.

Summary

This chapter has clarified what determines an assertive trainer, and how you measure up to this by:

- defining your own objectives for assertiveness
- looking at the benefits to you of using assertiveness
- asking you to do some self-assessment
- examining some of the hurdles which may make assertiveness difficult for you
- looking at six case studies for ideas and encouragement.

The next chapter looks at how assertiveness affects all aspects of training.

5 Training assertively

If assertiveness is accepted as being a valuable skill in training, it will influence every aspect, from the idea and identification of needs, through the delivery to the final evaluation.

This chapter looks at the influence of assertiveness on the design, setting up and delivery of training other than specific assertiveness courses:

- the assertive ground rules for training
- designing training assertively
- the influence of assertiveness on recruitment and publicity material
- the physical setting
- delivering training assertively
- dealing assertively with situations which trainers face

Additional aspects of the setting up and delivery of assertiveness courses are covered in Chapter 6.

The assertive ground rules for training

These ground rules form a foundation set of values and beliefs which flavour every aspect of the training. All of them are already good training practice, but may place the emphasis on a different aspect from traditional training.

Believe in assertiveness

As Colin Russell makes clear in his case study, training assertively takes a lot more commitment from the trainer than just understanding the definition and using a set of skills when on show. When assertiveness is practised really well, it becomes a philosophy and approach for building and maintaining relationships. Truly demonstrating self-respect and respect for others may mean changing old habits and practices in the course room, and so trainers have to do more than just think that it seems like a good idea—they also have to believe in the implications.

Demonstrate equality

To demonstrate self-respect and respect for others implies balanced, equal relationships. This does not mean that trainers have to like everyone equally, or treat everyone anonymously to ensure equal treatment.

Trainers are in positions of authority in the course room, but it's important to remember that, although the trainer may have more knowledge or advanced skills than the participants on a specific subject, they are there as equals and need to treat everyone with equal respect. Assertiveness transcends boundaries. This means:

- treating everyone equally as human beings. So the 16-year-old who started in the organization last week is treated with as much respect and dignity as an individual as the senior manager with 30 years' experience.
- being able to take account of and understand people who differ in gender, race and culture, physical abilities, age, social standing, level in the organization, religion or sexual preference.
- believing that, despite people's differences, they all have an equal right to their opinions and feelings.
- that your opinions and feelings are also important.
- challenging assertively any prejudices and assumptions which are demonstrated by participants. You will also need to know your organization's equal opportunities policy really well in case you are challenged on it.
- examining your own prejudices and assumptions.

It's their course As a trainer, you are not there to provide light entertainment for a day or two. Nor are the participants there to jump through hoops to please you. It is a partnership between you and the group. Sadly, there are still anecdotes told of trainers who seem to regard a training event as an opportunity to manipulate, show off, or indulge in an 'ego trip' at the participants' expense.

This means:

- the organization's needs have to be met
- the needs of the group need to be addressed in a way which they can use and to which they can relate
- you should avoid telling your favourite story regardless of whether it's appropriate or doing a particular exercise because it's fun to watch
- really listening to the participants
- using their real-life examples and issues
- ensuring that the participants have enough space and time to raise their issues
- not going on to 'auto pilot'—especially if it's a course with which you're very familiar

Self-nomination Bullying, ordering or manipulating someone to attend a course against their will is not assertive. It is also ineffective if the course is of a development nature, as the individual needs to accept responsibility for their own development, and making the decision whether or not to attend the training is an important step in accepting that responsibility. The suggestions which follow apply to training in which the individual has a choice whether or not to attend. There is also a great deal of compulsory training, such as culture change programmes, legal or financial courses, health and safety and skills courses, so it is accepted that this ground rule is not always enforceable. However, the assertive trainer will put up a case for self-nomination, knowing that it will achieve better results. This means:

- ensuring that publicity material clearly explains that the course is self-nominating
- having some way of checking, early in the course, that no one is there against their will
- having a strategy to deal with managers who are sending people against their will, if the course is self-nominating
- accepting the possibility of aggressive or passive behaviour from people who have been sent against their will
- letting people drop out of the course, if they really don't want to be there

Confidentiality

Confidentiality is a way of demonstrating respect for others and is especially important where issues of a personal or sensitive nature will be raised; a safe situation needs to be provided.

This means:

- clarifying beforehand whether your client or organization accepts confidentiality for the course or whether they will be expecting a report back on what happened
- agreeing a contract of confidentiality with the group. This cannot be imposed—individuals have to make their own decision
- taking assertive action with an individual or group if you discover or suspect that the confidentiality has been broken
- assertively respecting the confidentiality when other people ask you for information about the group or individuals (a useful guideline for this is that only information about attendance record is fed back. This needs to be clear with the group)

Accept people as they are

As assertiveness involves respect for others, it follows that it also involves accepting where they are in their lives, their opinions and beliefs. It does not mean having to agree with them, or not wanting to influence or change those life patterns or beliefs.

This means:

- accepting the reality of people's behaviour
- accepting people's right to hold their own opinions and beliefs
- knowing where you stand in relation to these
- realizing the effect of these on you
- openly expressing your own thoughts and feelings
- not passing judgement

Stay positive

When there is cynicism, manipulation, sarcasm, violence or any other form of negative behaviour, it can be tempting to fight fire with fire, abandon assertiveness, resort to aggression or passively give up.

Assertiveness is essentially an optimistic approach to life and training.

This means:

- assertively challenging negative behaviours and bringing them out into the open
- making sure that feedback is given constructively and that time is given for it to sink in
- suggesting possible actions to be taken
- accepting that they may reject your suggestions or feedback
- resisting the temptation to make a clever comment at someone else's expense

Build people up— don't knock them down

Sadly, we often meet people who have had very negative experiences of training because the trainer or the process had taken them apart, knocking their self-confidence and resulting in them feeling destroyed. This is aggressive training and is worryingly prevalent. It may have been unintentional, from an inexperienced or insensitive trainer, or intentional, from trainers who get their satisfaction out of humiliating participants and may even believe that 'it's good for them'. Assertiveness in training does not mean running a 'cosy' course because building people up involves stretching and challenging, which may well make the trainer unpopular and the participants uncomfortable.

This means:

- building people up from where they are
- stretching them to achieve more by building on what they already do or have
- encouraging positive changes in skills and behaviour
- challenging a co-trainer's behaviour if you experience it as negative
- giving lots of assertive feedback
- encouraging people to do more than they believe possible
- praising and complimenting people as well as criticizing

Encourage action

The fourth ingredient in assertiveness (say specifically what you want to happen) moves people into the future. So it is on courses. However enjoyable and useful the training, it's important to build links with the reality which participants will face after the course.

This means:

- having a formal action planning session at the end of every course
- using realistic and relevant examples throughout
- giving real examples from your own experience
- building in practical sessions
- before the course, being clear what expectations the client/organization has
- constantly asking participants, 'What can you do about this?' throughout the course

No magic answers If you are running a course involving technical, legal, financial or procedural content, there will be right and wrong answers. However, any course involving behaviours, inter-personal skills in any shape or form, or a developmental element cannot give set or magic answers. However, the aggressive trainer will, of course, know all the answers!

This means:

- expressing your own opinion and views clearly
- accepting that participants will not always accept your opinions and views
- encouraging participants to decide on whatever is most effective and relevant for them
- not being drawn into giving a magic answer
- accepting that what works for one person may not work for another
- restraining the participants from giving each other magic answers

Further ground rules specifically for assertiveness training are outlined in the next chapter.

Designing training assertively

Assertiveness can be applied right from the beginning when training needs are first identified, through the structure and content of courses, preparation of handouts, design and choice of exercises, videos and films and the use of video recorders.

Analysing training needs assertively The purpose of a training needs analysis is to ensure that there is accurate collection of all the information which will lead to correct diagnosis of the real needs of an individual or group, as opposed to the 'felt' need. Clark (1991) discriminates between the collection of hard and soft information, for example:

Hard	Soft
Organization structures	Opinions
Agendas	Perceptions
Minutes of meetings	Feelings
Recorded decisions	Behaviour
Procedures	Relationships
Systems	
Statistics	
Policy/marketing decisions	
Technical changes	

In addition there may be, for skills training for example, other hard information such as production and sales figures, customer complaints, times spent on particular duties, and so on and soft information such as intuited needs, or impressions.

Questions used in the analysis of training needs should reflect the nature of the information to be gathered, for example:

- **questions to encourage people to say what they think**
  What are your views on . . .?
  What do you think should be done about . . .?
- **questions to encourage people to say what they feel**
  How do you feel about . . .?
  What are your feelings on . . .?
- **questions to elicit specific information**
  How often does this have to be done?
  Who else is involved in this decision?
  When, exactly, do the mistakes occur?
- **questions to check accuracy of facts**
  Does this ever happen more than five times per year?
  Are you, your manager and the receptionist the only people involved?

Assertive design of courses

Overall good design of courses needs:

- clarity of objectives
- content related to the objectives
- rhythms or patterns of the days, so that participants can settle and know where they are
- a good balance and design of different types of activities to address different learning styles

Clarity of objectives

Assertive objectives are:

- specific, so that all are clear what is expected
- achievable by the majority, and not set so high that only a few participants stand any chance of achieving them
- measurable, so that there is a means of discerning degrees of achievement
- positive in the way they are written so that they encourage positive outcomes rather than negative ones: encourage a new habit rather than break down an old one, for example
- developmental and stretching, so that the participants are encouraged to reach for higher performances and abilities
- action orientated, so that people know what it is that they are expected to do

In training courses or longer programmes where, within broad guidelines, participants are encouraged to set their own objectives, they may need varying degrees of support or challenge to enable them to set realistic objectives.

Content related to the objectives

Any course material that does not relate to the objectives is usually there either because the trainer has passively been unable to tell the client or sponsor that the particular pet theme of theirs doesn't belong, or because the trainer is being manipulative in sliding in some material which is not needed to achieve the objectives. So beware the temptation to include favourite sessions when they are not needed.

Rhythm or pattern to the day

Often in their daily lives people have a pattern or rhythm to the day. On training courses they have to conform to the pattern set by the trainer. If there is to be respect for each other the pattern set needs to be:

- achievable by the group
- at a pace that will stimulate the participants
- healthy and not putting people under enormous strain or in a sub-servient role

Unassertive trainers have been known to keep people up late working when they are obviously well beyond their limits of effectiveness.

Activities to suit learning styles

Honey and Mumford (1986) describe the four learning styles:

- **activists**, who learn from doing and therefore like new, exciting experiences where they have high visibility and few constraints—they generally plunge in to get on with things
- **pragmatists**, who need to be convinced that the learning is relevant and practical. They learn from role models, examples, practising with coaching, simulation and concentrating on practical issues
- **theorists**, who learn best from understanding the overlying structure, system, model, concept or theory. They need time to question and probe, be stretched intellectually and like participating in complex situations. They learn best when they can see the logic and order in an idea
- **reflectors**, who need time to observe what is happening, think about it and review what has happened. They like to take their time over things and produce carefully considered analyses. Their learning takes place over the following days.

Most people, including trainers, have a mixture of all four learning styles. It is not always practical to check each person's learning style before a piece of training, so the assertive trainer ensures that all four learning styles are catered for and that in judging how people's responses to training situations, they take account of how much the participant's learning style may be influencing the results they see. Showing respect for all the learning styles means designing courses which do not favour one learning style over the others. Designing training in the image of your own preferred learning style is aggressive and puts down the other styles, as well as being poor training practice.

Materials and exercises

There is little point in trainers behaving assertively, demonstrating self-respect and respect for others if the materials and exercises on their courses are sending out a contradictory message.

If you are required to deliver a set course in a standard way, using standard materials and exercises which you regard as unassertive, then, as always, you have a choice. Assertive trainers will raise the concerns with their managers or clients to explore alternatives; maybe using different materials and exercises, taking a different approach, and, if they feel their integrity is being compromised, refusing to deliver the course in an unacceptable way.

Check the implications and tone of:

- handouts
- exercises
- videos/films/open learning materials
- the use of camcorders or video cameras

Handouts   Handouts can easily become out of date or express views and assumptions which are irrelevant or even offensive.

Ensure that your handouts:

- include examples from different genders, races, ages and experiences
- have illustrations or cartoons which include different types of people
- have jokes or cartoons which are not at the expense of any particular group(s) or individual(s)
- respect different views
- do not put a person or group of people down
- have practical relevance to each group of participants
- acknowledge sources

Exercises   Exercises are vital to help participants practise in a supportive environment. Not only does the exercise itself need to give support and respect to the individuals, but also the way the exercise is briefed and debriefed; we look at this later in the chapter.

Ensure that the content and design of your exercises:

- do not humiliate anyone
- do not require anyone to become a victim
- do not encourage passive or aggressive behaviour
- do not cast people in roles
- enable people to build on their existing level of skill
- build people up
- challenge stereotypes
- are as realistic as possible
- respect the different learning styles

Videos, films and open learning materials   Ensure that any videos, films, books or any other learning materials are in tune with the positive and assertive messages coming from you and the rest of your course material.

For example: a leadership course attended by both men and women went very well until, in conclusion, a film was shown to recap the main learning points. Unfortunately, in the film, all the leadership roles were taken by men, whilst women were sidelined into peripheral support roles. This successfully insulted the women, reinforced stereotypes, and undermined the 'you can do it' message of the previous two days.

If learning materials come highly recommended, or if they have been used for some time, it's easy to become complacent. Take another look at the films, videos or any other materials which you use or are considering using. It's not good enough to just make an apology or joke about unassertive materials before using them. You are still responsible for their content.

Ensure that:

- aggressive or passive behaviour is not being modelled or promoted
- jokes are not at someone else's expense
- a wide range of different types of people are shown in different roles
- the messages are positive and encourage action
- the material is really essential to the course
- you're not using it to make *you* feel better

Camcorders and video cameras

Camcorders and video cameras are increasingly used in training, especially on courses on communication skills such as interviewing techniques or public speaking. If used properly, they can be a very valuable source of feedback and can enable the participants to extend their learning. If used badly or inappropriately, they can be intrusive, irrelevant and humiliating.

The assertive trainer checks that:

- a camcorder or video camera is really necessary—consider gaining the feedback in other ways
- everyone on the course understands how, why and when the camcorder or video camera is going to be used
- no-one is videoed without their permission
- the use of a camcorder or video camera is known about beforehand—maybe in the pre-course publicity or joining instructions
- they are available to talk with anyone who has concerns about being videoed
- the feedback is strictly controlled and videos are not used gratuitously
- the videotape is, ideally, given to the participant to take away afterwards or, alternatively, wiped clean to ensure confidentiality

Publicity material

Assertively written recruitment and publicity materials will be open, truthful and give plenty of specific information about the course, its objectives and for whom it's designed. It will also give realistic outcomes and expectations for the training. Assertively written recruitment and publicity material will not manipulate or trick people into attending, give misleading information, omit information, create unrealistic expectations, or make unrealistic claims for the training.

The physical setting

The choice of room and the type and position of furniture all influence whether a course is run assertively or not. Although much training is conducted outside a training room (outdoor training, open learning, home study, etc.) it is still the case that a great deal of training happens either on-site or off-site in some form of room, with furniture!

The importance of body language and body space was outlined in Chapter 2. The layout and use of furniture is an extension of those principles. By the positioning and choice of furniture, the trainer can immediately create an atmosphere that says:

'I'm in charge, I'm superior to you lot' or
'I'm going to keep you at a distance so I feel less threatened' or
'I feel OK about myself and about you and we're going to work together.'

Tables

Tables immediately create barriers and create a 'schoolroom' atmosphere with the trainer in charge. If you really must have a table on which to put your notes, glass of water, or whatever, then place it beside you or, even better, behind you so you are in direct contact with the participants. Sitting behind a table formalizes the atmosphere, placing you in a superior position with participants in an inferior role. It will discourage interaction, because it is the layout most used at formal conferences.

With the increase of the sophisticated technology associated with training, some of the newest training centres have tables which are fixed to the floor: they are permanently wired up with video or computer controls, dimmers for the lights, and even electronically operated curtains and screens. Even though you can't move this type of table, you can move around to the front of it, so that technology doesn't take over.

Think twice about the participants having tables, and provide them only if they are absolutely essential. When participants have their own tables to hide behind, it is easier for them to use habitual passive or aggressive behaviour. If you decide that tables are essential because of the amount of material or paperwork involved, make a special effort to move the participants away from the tables for any group discussion or practical work.

Chairs

In addition to the positioning of tables, chairs can also enhance or impair your ability to behave assertively. More often than not there will be no choice at all in the type of chair, as most training centres and hotels only have one type available—bought in bulk. However, if there is choice, ensure that the trainer's chair is the same as the participants' and that no one is physically higher or lower than anyone else.

For example: when a trainer arrived at an Arts Centre to run a one-day workshop on leadership, she discovered that the room allocated was the coffee lounge which had fixed, very low, kidney-shaped settees for the participants and no chair at all for herself. She spent the morning struggling to draw out twelve participants who were virtually lying flat on their backs in order to see the trainer who was left standing. The workshop only came to life when the trainer insisted that they moved to a corner of the canteen with less luxurious chairs which enabled eye contact and equality between trainer and participants.

For example: a facilitators' workshop was allocated to the boardroom of a major organization as it was the only room available that day. Although they were able to move away from the boardroom table, the two trainers felt intimidated all day by the fifteen participants sitting in enormous highbacked leather armchairs!

Maria Pemberton reminds us that participants' levels of concentration seriously deteriorate after only 20 minutes (Pemberton, 1982). This is further significantly reduced if they are uncomfortable or in any form of pain. Whatever chairs you use, they will never be comfortable for everyone all the time and, however interesting your training is, a painful back or numb bottom will be a very effective distraction!

The assertive trainer encourages people to do whatever they need to do to ease discomforts or pain. This might involve finding a different chair, bringing a foam wedge or pillow, resting feet on some form of support (books or a briefcase), standing up, sitting on the floor or even lying down.

Trainers who insist on everyone sitting in a particular way are imposing their wishes on the group and have moved into using aggressive behaviour.

Room layout If a rectangular room is being used, it is usually laid up in the traditional theatre style shown in Figure 5.1. This clearly places the trainer in a position of authority, and the participants lapse into passivity. To support your own assertiveness and create a more equal relationship, move the trainer's position, push the table back and curve the rows (see Figure 5.2).

Also consider where you place other items, such as overhead projectors and especially cameras and camcorders. If the first thing participants see on entering the room is a conspicuous camera or camcorder at the front of the room, it reinforces the 'I know something you don't know' superior role of the trainer. Tuck it in a corner until you need it, and then preface its use with an open explanation of how and why you are using it

Delivering training assertively

Having researched and prepared the training with care for all the skills and philosophy of assertiveness, it becomes a key skill in the actual delivery of the training.

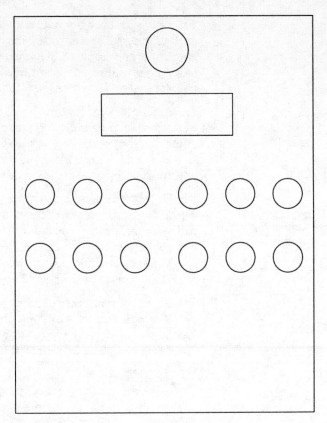

Figure 5.1 *Theatre style*

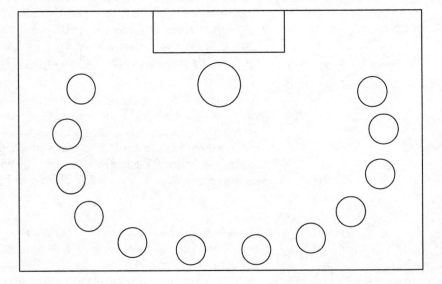

Figure 5.2 *Amended style*

Using the five ingredients

The application of the five ingredients of assertiveness is seen in trainers who:

Listen
- give time on their courses for some discussion
- encourage the expression of differing views
- are non-judgemental in receiving differing views
- are attentive to everything that is being said
- are sensitive to the feelings being expressed, as well as the words
- take others' opinions seriously
- give direct eye contact
- remain open to differing opinions

Demonstrate that they understand
- do not dismiss or denigrate anything or anyone
- reveal some of their own experience
- ask relevant, direct questions
- say if they *don't* understand
- do not make assumptions
- are prepared to become vulnerable
- treat people as equals
- are flexible enough to adjust the course content or process to make it more relevant if necessary

Say what they think and feel
- *know* what they think and feel
- express their thoughts and feelings openly
- include thoughts and feelings of a personal nature
- are not embarrassed to reveal feelings
- are prepared to be seen as human beings, not impersonal automatons
- are able to express negative feelings

Say specifically what they want to happen
- do not impose their wishes on participants
- are clear about what they want
- are able to be flexible in achieving what they want

Consider the consequences of joint solutions
- will take the time to discuss joint solutions when necessary
- are open to alternatives
- have alternatives to offer
- do not regard it as a failure if the participants do not do exactly what the trainer wished

Key elements in training

While recognizing that many of these suggestions will be seen as good training practice anyway, consider to what extent your assertiveness is demonstrated in these key elements. Most trainers can be vigilant with their assertiveness in formal sessions in training, but are more vulnerable with spontaneous or informal remarks.

Examples and anecdotes
In addition to short examples that may be given to elaborate on points, most trainers have their own selection of stories or anecdotes which bring human interest points and make the learning more relevant to

individual situations. Assertive examples and anecdotes:

- are true
- fit the session
- have only enough detail to make the point
- avoid being an 'ego trip' for the trainer
- credit the originator
- acknowledge the participants' experience and opinions

Asides and jokes   Part of the liveliness of any course is contained in the quick asides and jokes that take place. These are usually spontaneous and fun, and in addition, to be assertive they will:

- be handled with care
- avoid putting people or groups of people down
- suit the humour of the group, and not that of the trainer
- not wound or offend participants
- not diminish people who are not there to defend themselves
- not be sarcastic

Questions   Good training practice demands that trainers understand how to deal with and use questions effectively, that they know the difference between teaching questions and testing questions, that they are able to ask open questions and closed questions, and know when to use each type. Being assertive with questions means being aware of which ingredient of assertiveness is being used when particular types of questions are asked.

For example: in listening, questions are asked to clarify facts, and to gain a full picture. In demonstrating understanding, questions are asked to fill in gaps in understanding. If you know that participants have not been stating clearly what they think or feel, then use questions to elicit their thoughts and feelings. Questions can also help participants to state what it is that they want to happen. When looking at the consequences of joint solutions, most questions begin with 'What if . . .?' Only by looking at the 'What if . . .?' in relation to everyone involved will the full consequences become clear, and lead to a decision.

Questions can also direct the flow of conversation and events, so the person asking the questions can have more power than the person answering them. Assertive trainers share power with their participants and use questions to enhance the participants' learning, rather than to enhance the trainer's position.

Responding to questions is a matter of attaining the balance between having all the answers, if you happen to be the expert on the subject, and allowing the participants to have their answers too. There is also a balance between always having to have an answer for every question that's asked of you, and pretending that you know nothing, or that your views are not important.

One of the ground rules at the beginning of this chapter is, 'It's their course': participants' questions are very important. There is a danger of passing questions back to the group to enable a group discussion, while never coming off the fence and giving your own views, so a balance has to be struck between these two as well.

Role play, practice, and exercises

Participants on development programmes often look for the catch or trick in exercises. This is usually because they have experienced that some trainers design and run training activities which catch out participants and undermine their confidence and achievements. As a result, participants feel manipulated and are mistrustful the next time they're on a course.

Check that in your briefing, facilitating and debriefing of exercises and roleplay you:

- ask for volunteers to undertake key tasks whenever possible
- assertively explain the need for volunteers if there are none!
- accept someone's refusal to do an exercise only after an assertive conversation with them
- explain why the exercise is important and what they will learn
- express your own feelings and thoughts about how the exercise is going or has gone
- stop someone becoming a scapegoat or a martyr in the debrief
- stop groups ganging up on each other or on an individual in the debrief
- encourage the use of the five assertive ingredients in the debrief even when it isn't an assertiveness course
- do not give examples at someone else's expense, however valuable the learning point
- don't laugh at or belittle people's efforts
- give guidelines on how to give and receive feedback, however briefly
- do not keep reminding the group of an individual's or group's mistake
- give clear, unambiguous and consistent briefs
- check understanding of the brief
- are prepared to see different interpretations

Assertiveness with participants

The response which you receive to your assertive behaviour will influence your ability to maintain it, especially in the early days. An aggressive, passive or assertive response makes different demands on the trainer.

Directly aggressive

At least you know this is happening! The group or person may be sarcastic, cynical, offensive, verbally violent or even physically violent. All the assertiveness ingredients are important here, but especially listening and demonstrating any understanding that you have with them. Participants behaving aggressively are often expecting or even hoping for a verbal fight with you, and you can be totally disarmed by your own openness and willingness to discuss joint solutions. Ask them what they specifically want from you and be clear in your own mind what you are prepared to do. This might be anything from allowing them not to do an exercise to letting them drop out of the course.

Indirectly aggressive   This is more difficult to deal with, because by definition it is not easy to know that it is happening. You may suspect this behaviour is being used by the atmosphere, by reluctance to participate in exercises, by muttered sarcastic remarks behind your back or by groups or individuals pretending not to hear you. It needs to be challenged as quickly as possible, with lots of expression of your own feelings and what you want to happen. Insist on the group or individual explaining their feelings and what they want to happen. It's unlikely that this will be resolved at the first attempt, and you may have to persist. Groups or individuals using indirect aggression do not expect to have it brought into the open, and may either sneer at or respect your own openness.

Passive   The group or person behaving passively can also be challenging to deal with, because, again, you often don't know it's happening. This is the group who quietly comply with everything you've asked of them, but don't tell you that they're getting nothing out of the course, exercise or activity, or that they don't understand it. Groups like this can turn aggressive afterwards, releasing their notches by writing a damning evaluation which makes you wonder whether you were in the same room on the same day! Alternatively, they may go away confused or dissatisfied and be reluctant to participate in further training. To help groups or individuals move from passivity towards assertiveness means again that all ingredients are needed, especially saying how you think and feel and saying what you specifically want to happen. People often cast the trainer in the role of an unfeeling automaton, and it can jolt them into a response when they hear: 'I'm feeling very uncomfortable at your lack of response and I need to know what your reaction is to the last exercise.' Christine Baines bears this out in her case study (see pages 69–70).

Assertive   The group or person behaving assertively is mostly a joy to work with, and becomes challenging and stretching for the trainer only if you find it difficult to handle their assertively telling you that they don't agree or don't want to do what you've asked them to do! If you do, you can assertively acknowledge it, express your feelings and repeat your request. It may be that they hadn't understood you properly the first time. Ultimately, once you've reassured yourself that they've properly considered your request, you can either move on to exploring a joint solution or assertively respect their opinion or decision.

Assertiveness with co-trainers   Dealing assertively with participants is one matter but having to deal assertively with your co-trainer (if you have one) can be quite another!

A good co-training relationship requires trust and respect between trainers. If both of you are working on your assertiveness with each other, this does not make it easy: it will mean sorting out difficulties between you openly and sometimes painfully, but it will give you a sound foundation on which to run the course.

If you are working with someone who does not behave assertively, and does not demonstrate trust and respect, then it puts the responsibility on you to raise these issues. A co-trainer's lack of assertiveness or resistance to your being assertive can be due to a wide range of reasons which can be aggravated if they know a little about assertiveness themselves. It may be that:

- they are cynical about assertiveness
- they don't really understand it (although they think they do)
- they regard themselves as perfectly assertive already (which often means that they behave aggressively)
- they regard themselves as more experienced than you
- they've been training for 25 years and don't see the need for assertiveness
- they've been manipulated by other trainers before and believe that manipulation and aggression is assertive
- they regard the use of assertiveness as being relevant only on assertiveness courses
- they've been unable to receive previous feedback on their lack of assertiveness

If you work regularly with the same co-trainer then you can take a long-term view in your assertive behaviour with them. You can give feedback at the end of the course, being clear about the changes you'd prefer for next time.

If you are thrown in with a co-trainer at short notice for just one or two courses, then your assertiveness will have to have immediate effect and feedback may have to be given whilst the course is in progress, which will be more risky.

Some hints and tips on dealing with co-trainers assertively follow:

Do:
- agree beforehand on some ground rules for your working relationship
- raise beforehand any issues with which you feel uncomfortable
- agree beforehand how you are going to deal with any disagreements during the training
- discover how your co-trainer prefers to receive feedback, if at all
- explain how you want to receive feedback
- listen to and respect your co-trainer's experience
- stand up for the sessions that you believe in, and that you do well
- encourage each other
- give credit to your co-trainer in public
- sort out disagreements in private

- be interested in what your co-trainer is doing or saying
- give them credit for their contribution
- build on your co-trainer's material
- give each other feedback afterwards
- listen to uncomfortable feedback

Don't:
- let them take your best sessions away from you
- belittle their experience
- ignore them or their session
- overrun your agreed time
- contradict your co-trainer in public
- interrupt
- stand in front of them or 'upstage' them in any way
- let your own feelings of discomfort go unexpressed
- distract the participants
- give negative feedback just as they're starting a session or at times when they are not able to discuss it

This is the ideal—something to work towards. It may take a lot of courage and several assertive conversations to achieve, but it is well worth while, as it will result in a more productive and supportive working relationship.

Assertiveness with guest speakers

Guest speakers can be the highlight of the course, bringing the subject matter to life, reinforcing all the learning points and inspiring the participants to action. Alternatively, they can disrupt the course by arriving late, disregard the briefing they've received and in their talk, undermine the work already achieved, leaving participants confused and negative and the trainers with a frantic patch-up job on their hands!

However clear the brief, however appropriate the person chosen and however brilliantly they did the session last time, guest speakers are the greatest unknown quantity and are the occasions when trainers have least control. Assertiveness is a key skill in maintaining control and maximizing the positive benefit of the guest speaker. This can be complicated if the guest speaker is more senior or in any way has more authority than the trainer. It takes courage to assertively ask the chief executive or famous celebrity to conclude when they've run over their allotted time! Assertiveness is helpful before, during and after the guest speaker's session.

Before
- a very clear brief (either written or spoken) outlining specifically what you want from them
- checking their understanding of the brief
- considering any additions or alterations to the brief
- explaining the context of the session and the overall course objectives
- agreeing exactly how you will run the session, who does what, timings, whether there will be questions, etc.

- agreeing how you will signal time checks or 'conclude' if necessary
- agreeing how the guest speaker will be introduced
- listening to and addressing their concerns

During
- explaining the objective of the guest speaker's session
- introducing the guest speaker as agreed
- positioning yourself so you do not distract from the guest speaker (aggressive) or make it difficult to regain control of the session (passive)
- being attentive to what the guest speaker is saying
- being attentive to the response of participants
- requesting the speaker to finish, using the previously agreed signal
- running the whole session in the manner previously agreed
- letting the guest speaker have their say, even if they directly contradict you
- being clear on which questions are or are not relevant
- allowing questions (if time allows)

Afterwards with the guest speaker
- asking them how they felt it went
- explaining how you felt it went
- giving feedback on the effectiveness of the session
- asking for specific changes or inclusions for next time (if relevant)
- thanking them for coming!

Afterwards with the participants and after the guest speaker has gone
If the session has gone well and on the whole was positive, no further action is needed. However, if you feel that the participants are upset, angry or confused, or if you think that your own position or opinion has been undermined or attacked:

- ask the group what they thought or felt about the guest speaker's session
- encourage specific examples and assertive feedback. Even if the participants do not know anything about assertiveness, give guidelines to encourage the use of the assertive ingredients by asking questions such as: 'What do you think about the session?', 'What are you feeling about it now?', 'What do you want to do about it?', 'What is your understanding of what was said or done?'
- assertively express your own thoughts and feelings about the session, without belittling the guest speaker or their views
- acknowledge that the guest speaker is entitled to her or his views
- encourage participants to clarify their own views

Colin Russell's anecdote (in his case study, pages 70–74) of dealing with a senior manager who contributed as a guest speaker on a management development programme is an excellent example of the importance of assertiveness in these often tricky situations.

Dealing assertively with situations which trainers face

The five assertiveness ingredients outlined in Chapter 2 are the basis for all assertive behaviour. They give enough guidelines for most situations, and need to be practised first. However, some specific situations require an adaptation to, or departure from, these basic steps. This section looks at when you:

- are asked for straight information
- find inconsistency in someone's behaviour
- need a response from someone
- haven't been listened to, or aren't being taken notice of
- are dealing with someone's strong feelings
- have strong feelings yourself
- want to say 'no'
- need to give criticism
- need to receive criticism
- need to give or receive a compliment

Any of these situations could crop up with participants, co-trainers, managers, guest-speakers, whole groups, individuals, anyone with whom the assertive trainer deals. Much of the material in this section is taken from the *Springboard Workbook* (Willis and Daisley, 1994).

When you are asked for straight information

This situation may seem straightforward enough, but it can easily slide into aggressive or passive behaviour. **For example**:

'How long do we have for the tea break?'

Passive reply:

'Well, I suggested 20 minutes, if that's OK by you?'

Aggressive reply:

'I've already said 20 minutes at least three times—why don't you concentrate?'

The assertive reply is short and informative:

'20 minutes'

When you find inconsistency in someone's behaviour

The inconsistency may be when:

- someone's body language contradicts what they're saying
- someone says one thing and does another
- the formal policy says one thing and the usual practice is another

Assertiveness accepts that life is full of inconsistencies but challenges them by:

- pointing out the inconsistency
- explaining the effect on you of the inconsistency
- saying what you want to happen

For example: 'You said you would support my new programme of courses, but I notice that there is no one from your department enrolled. I feel let down and annoyed about this and I'd like to know exactly what your view is.'

When you need a response from someone

Silence is common to all behaviours, but is the result of different causes. In passive behaviour, silence is because people:

- do not think their feelings or opinions are relevant or worth expressing
- are unable to work out what they are feeling or thinking
- are frightened of expressing their view in case they offend
- need time to think

In directly aggressive behaviour, silence is because the person is ignoring you or deliberately being difficult. In indirectly aggressive behaviour, the person does not want to openly express their views as they want to subvert your opinion or authority covertly. In assertive behaviour, silence is because the person has nothing to say.

To discover what is happening, a response is required. The assertive approach is to make very specific requests to individuals. **For example**:

'Now that I've outlined what I mean by confidentiality for this course, I need to know how you feel about this before I move on.'

or

'I know we've heard from Tom and Joan on where they stand on this issue but I'd also like to know your opinion.'

This is especially important when dealing with indirect aggression, as gaining a response makes it more difficult for people to sabotage by saying afterwards, 'Well, of course, I never agreed with that'.

When you aren't being listened to, or aren't being taken notice of

When you suspect that you're not being listened to, the tendency is to move to either aggressive or passive behaviour by shouting or giving up. The assertive response is to simply repeat key parts of your message whilst listening carefully and continuing to acknowledge the other person's view. If this takes some time, you may also want to express your frustration at not being listened to.

For example: you have told the course administrator that you need the participants list on Tuesday:

Course administrator: 'Yeah, yeah. I'll see what I can do.'
You: 'I know you're busy, but I really do need that list on Tuesday morning.'
Course administrator: 'Well, we'll see—I'll do my best.'
You: 'I'm sure you will but I actually need that list in my hand on Tuesday morning.'
... and so on.

When you are dealing with someone's strong feelings

When people have very strong feelings they tend to either express them at the expense of others (aggressive behaviour) or bottle them up because they're scared that the feelings will overwhelm them or that expressing them will make the situation worse (passive behaviour).

Either way, assertive behaviour helps to bring the true feelings out in the open so you can discover the reality of the situation and build on it. When dealing with strong feelings, the most important ingredients are listening (not only to words, but also to feelings and intentions) and demonstrating whatever understanding you have of the other person's feelings or situation.

When feelings are running high or when the situation is sensitive, it is even more important to truly demonstrate your understanding. This doesn't mean agreeing or colluding with the other person. Demonstrating understanding may be the only way to keep lines of communication open.

Strong feelings are often very difficult for people to express. They often don't say 'I'm very angry' or 'I feel deeply hurt', but it is conveyed through their appearance and voice. Acknowledging what you observe helps people to express their feelings and can also help to defuse the situation.

For example: a previously helpful participant has suddenly become very withdrawn and short tempered with you.

   You: 'You seem annoyed about something. What's the matter?'

When you have strong feelings yourself

It isn't always possible to think of reasonable and positive things to say, especially if you're feeling upset yourself. When this is the case, say so, remembering to:

● be very specific
● describe the behaviour which is affecting you, rather than blaming the other person for your feelings
● explain how their behaviour affects you
● say specifically what you want to happen

For example: 'I know you don't like losing staff time on training, but I am furious at your attacks on this year's training programmes in the meeting this morning. If you've got any comments to make, I'd prefer you to talk to me direct in future.'

When you want to say 'no'

Someone's ability to say a straight 'no' to a request depends on a variety of factors, including the culture in which they've been brought up. When working with mixed nationality groups, it is noticeable that people from some nationalities squirm with the difficulty of pronouncing this small word, while people from other backgrounds look on in amazement, having no difficulty at all.

Assertive behaviour enables a straight 'no' plus a short, straightforward explanation if you wish. When people first come to assertiveness they usually manage this and then ruin the effect by following it up with an apology or elaborate justification to soften the blow of their refusal.

For example:

> Participant: 'Could you give me some advice on my situation over lunch today?'
> Passive: 'Well, I don't know. The lunch break is the only time I've got to catch my breath, and I've got to make some phone calls. I'm sorry to seem unhelpful.'
> Aggressive: 'Certainly not! I'm far too busy!'
> Assertive: 'No' plus assertive explanation only if you wish, such as: 'No, I don't have any spare time today.'

When you need to give criticism

Many people avoid giving criticism as it can be uncomfortable. People who use passive behaviour avoid it altogether, people who use indirect aggression give the criticism in the disguise of jokes, throw-away remarks or sarcastic put-downs, while people who use direct aggression just dump the criticism on people in such a way that only the really thick-skinned can cope with it.

There are five steps in giving criticism assertively:

1 Give specific examples of the behaviour you're criticizing
2 Say how you feel about it and the effect it has on you
3 Say what changes you'd prefer to see or hear
4 Listen to the response (words, voice and body language)
5 If necessary, work out a joint solution to take you into the future

For example: your co-trainer keeps interrupting your session with prompts.

> You: 'I know you're keen to build on my session, but when you constantly interrupt me in mid-session I am completely thrown and it undermines my confidence. If you've got anything to add I'd rather that you waited until I'd finished.'

When you need to receive criticism

Receiving feedback, especially negative feedback, well, enables you to assess your own behaviour and its effectiveness. However, it can be very difficult to remain open to the feedback without automatically defending yourself and fighting back (directly aggressive), agreeing (passive) or switching off (indirectly aggressive).

Remaining open, without agreeing or dismissing the feedback, is the most important aspect of receiving criticism. Most people are not very good at giving criticism, so to really understand them you may also have to ask specific questions about your behaviour and its effect. You do not have to agree or disagree.

There are four useful steps in receiving criticism:

1 Remain open—listen to what is being said and ask for specific examples to clarify your own understanding
2 Let the other person know you've heard and understood the criticism, by giving the other person your immediate response or by asking questions to clarify your understanding
3 Take time afterwards to decide: Is it all true? Is it partly true? Is it totally false? What do you want to do?
4 Change your behaviour afterwards if you want to

For example: 'I can see that the exercise was not helpful for everyone. I'm not sure how I feel about that at the moment and will give it some thought before next time.'

This aspect of assertiveness has particular relevance to receiving evaluation material and so is explored in greater detail in Chapter 7.

When you need to give or receive a compliment

Trainers are often cast in a role of authority by participants and, however much effort is used in trying to break down the barrier between trainer and participants, there is always the danger that the trainer is somehow regarded as less than human, so doesn't need the positive feedback which can give a welcome boost. It can be difficult for a participant to give a compliment as they may be concerned that it will look like 'crawling to teacher'. Equally, it can be difficult for trainers to receive compliments, however clumsily expressed, especially if they feel they haven't done a particularly good job that day.

- **To give a compliment**, keep it short and specific. Then shut up! If you go on about it, you could be seen as insincere.
- **To receive a compliment**, really listen to what's being said and acknowledge it. You may also want to say (briefly) how you feel. Don't push the compliment aside, run yourself down or interrupt the giver.

For example:

Participant: 'You've been marvellous on this course, it's been great.'
Passive: 'Oh well, I only did the easy bits—it's John's course really.'
Aggressive (sarcastic): 'Well, I'm glad someone noticed—it's been horrible for me all day.'
Assertive: 'Thanks—I'm glad it's gone well.'

Assertiveness practice

To summarize this chapter and to put assertiveness theory into practice, Figure 5.3 gives ten situations with which trainers have to cope. Consider your own assertive response to each of these and write them in the space provided. Remember that there are no right or wrong answers, as different people will have different feelings about these situations and want different outcomes. The assertive answer will include the five assertiveness ingredients and additional ideas from this chapter.

1. Participants say strongly and angrily, in an opening plenary, that the training should be for their managers and not for them because it is the managers who cause the problems.
   You reply:

2. Your co-trainer regularly turns up only five minutes before the workshop is due to start, when you had both agreed to be there an hour before to set up. When you ask the reason for his/her lateness, there is no specific reason.
   You say:

3. A participant raises an issue specific to themselves with a guest speaker who has been partly responsible for the relevant policy. After the speaker has given a generalized response, the participant persists and is taking up a lot of time.
   You say:

4. Your co-trainer twice runs over their time, leaving you with too little time to do your session properly.
   Raise this with your co-trainer:

5. Going around small groups who are supposed to be doing a practical exercise, you discover a group who have decided that they prefer having a discussion and are not doing the exercise.
   You say:

Figure 5.3 Questionnaire

6. During a sensitive part of your course, a loud electric drill starts up in the room next door.
   You say to the participants:

   You say to the person using the electric drill:

7. Your co-trainer has handled a discussion in a way which you found patronizing. Tell him or her assertively:

8. A participant tells you that they have only enrolled on the course to have a day out of the office.
   You reply:

9. A manager telephones during the lunch break on your course to insist that one of the participants returns to the office immediately to help out.
   You say to the manager:

10. There is no vegetarian food available for lunch although it was ordered in advance.
    You say to the caterer:

Figure 5.3 (continued)

Summary

This chapter has outlined the relevance of assertiveness to many different aspects of training, especially the delivery, and has shown how the use of assertiveness by trainers enhances other training skills and techniques to improve the overall effectiveness of the trainer and the training.

The key points are:

- assertiveness is a key skill which enhances the effectiveness of any training
- it is especially relevant for courses containing any communication, inter-personal skills or developmental aspect
- being truly assertive requires the trainer not only to know the theory but also to believe in the philosophy of assertiveness
- trainers need to practise assertiveness
- assertiveness has relevance in all stages and aspects of training

The final stage of training, which has not been outlined in this chapter, is that of evaluation. As assertiveness is especially useful in gaining accurate evaluation material, it is covered in detail in Chapter 7.

References

Clark, N. (1991) *Managing Personal Learning and Change*, McGraw-Hill, Maidenhead.

Honey, P. and Mumford, A. (1986) *The Manual of Learning Styles*, Honey, Maidenhead.

Pemberton, Maria (1982) *Effective Speaking*, The Industrial Society, London.

Willis, Liz and Daisley, Jenny (1994) *Springboard Womens Development Workbook*, 3rd edition, Hawthorn Press, Stroud.

6 Assertiveness courses

This chapter should not be looked at in isolation, as it works in conjunction with previous chapters. It considers aspects additional to those already covered in Chapter 5 which apply when running specific assertiveness training, either as a session in a larger course or as a course on its own. These are:

- further design considerations
- the importance of good publicity and in-house communication
- the trainer as role model

To conclude the chapter, there are case studies of five individuals who describe their own experience of attending assertiveness courses.

Further design considerations

When designing assertiveness training, in addition to all the usual issues, there are specific issues about:

- your target group
- on-site or off-site venues
- assertiveness as a stand-alone subject or with other training
- the length of the training

Your target group

Self-nomination

The ground rule of self-nomination outlined in Chapter 5 is of especial importance for assertiveness courses as it is not possible to help someone learn assertiveness if they don't want to. However, whilst no one should ever be sent on assertiveness training against their will, self-nomination does not exclude encouraging, cajoling, and suggesting that someone might attend. Without some encouragement and support, people using passive or aggressive behaviour will not be challenged in their view that they are already assertive!

Mixed-gender or single-gender groups?

The 1975 Sex Discrimination Act allows for single-gender training, under Section 47 covering training providers, Section 48 covering employers, Section 22 covering educational provision and Section 34 covering voluntary bodies.

Sections 47 and 48 state that single-gender training has to prove that the gender is absent or underrepresented in particular areas of work or occupational areas, and that the training offered will help that gender enter these areas of work. This also covers national or local shortages or underrepresentation in areas of work or occupational areas. Alternatively, single-gender training can be offered to people returning to an area of work or occupational area where their gender is absent or under-represented, after a period of time 'discharging domestic responsibilities'. The provisions under Sections 47 and 48 cover the women-into-management type of course which often include sessions on assertiveness.

Section 22 covers educational provision and allows single-gender training as long as 'separate but equal' courses are offered, giving both men and women equal access and equal opportunity to attend. The provisions under Section 22 would cover the men-only and women-only assertiveness courses offered publicly. A difficulty with this occurs if one of the courses is cancelled because there were only one or two people enrolled, as these few people would not then be being offered equal opportunity and equal access.

The Equal Opportunities Commission also states that:

Outside mainstream education, there is one other exception to the Act which could serve to legitimise the provision of single-sex courses. Section 34 of the Act permits men and women to set up and operate non-statutory, non-profit-making voluntary bodies whose membership and related benefits may be restricted to men only, or women only. Consequently, a single-sex voluntary body could lawfully provide for its members educational opportunities as part of its bona fide activities.

The legal situation on single-gender training is very complicated and so, before embarking on any single-gender training, you are recommended to contact The Equal Opportunities Commission at Overseas House, Quay Street, Manchester M3 3HN, telephone 061 833 9244, to talk through your ideas and prevent putting yourself at risk.

As the legislation is an added consideration, why bother with single-gender assertiveness courses at all? Single-gender courses are enormously valuable as part of an overall training strategy, as they provide a different training environment from a mixed-gender course. Many of these differences are of positive benefit, and some organizations offer assertiveness in women-only, men-only and mixed modules, so that the individual can choose whatever he or she finds most useful.

On women-only courses, women say (Willis and Daisley, 1994) that they:

- feel more confident
- are more free to be themselves
- feel more able to take risks
- believe that the course is more confidential
- believe that their learning was enhanced by the course being for women only

The other advantages were that:

- they heard a woman's point of view
- there were similar issues between the participants
- they could explore issues especially relevant to them

Trainers' observations of women-only training bear this out and also suggest that women:

- settle down more quickly ...
- work at a much deeper level ...
- trust and support each other more ...

... than when there are men present.

This is especially important on assertiveness courses as the real situations which women want to resolve often involve men. **For example**: various degrees of sexual harassment, verbal and physical violence, unwelcome jokes and comments and unhelpful assumptions. Women often say that if the course had included male participants they would not have attended at all.

There are also disadvantages to women-only training:

- only the women's point of view is presented
- the course does not mirror 'real life'
- men are deprived of an opportunity to learn from women's experience
- women are deprived of an opportunity to learn from men's experience

The anecdotal evidence gathered from male assertiveness trainers suggests that the advantages to women of women-only courses are not transferable to men on men-only courses. This may be because being in a single-gender group (especially at work) is not unusual for most men—they regard it as ordinary, so there is no special advantage. For those men who choose to use it, a men-only course does give the opportunity to raise and work on situations which they would not want to raise in a mixed-gender environment.

Mixed-gender assertiveness courses have the potential to become the best, or the worst, of both worlds!

Advantages of mixed-gender groups:

- may more accurately reflect people's lives
- enable women and men to understand each other better
- build relationships between men and women
- the women act as a stabilizing influence on the men

Disadvantages of mixed-gender groups:

- the women do not speak up
- the women may give their time and attention to the men
- the men may (consciously or unconsciously) take over
- greater danger of misunderstandings and distrust

- both genders 'play safe' and do not raise sensitive or important issues

Although assertiveness is now available for men-only and mixed-gender groups, most of the assertiveness training being run in the UK at the present is attended by women. Assertiveness has many benefits to both men and women and is also potentially very useful in building greater understanding between men and women. Fortunately, the level of interest in assertiveness by men is generally increasing as more men understand what assertiveness actually is and how it can be of benefit to them.

On-site or off-site? If you have no influence over the choice of venue, then obviously you'll make the best of whatever situation you find. However, the effectiveness of the best assertiveness course in the world will be hampered by a venue that does not have sufficient or appropriate space for groups to work in privacy. For assertiveness courses to work well, participants must feel secure enough to raise and practise their real situations, so the choice of venue is an important influence.

On-site advantages:

- familiar buildings
- familiar journey
- course has high visibility
- may be easier to organize than off-site
- family care arrangements are familiar
- cheaper

On-site disadvantages:

- easy to be interrupted
- course has high visibility
- tempting to slip back to work in the breaks
- difficult to behave differently
- difficult to raise personal issues
- familiarity can be threatening or too cosy
- difficult for the day(s) to be different from usual

Off-site advantages:

- gets people away from their usual environment
- significantly reduces the opportunities for interruptions
- keeps the group together during breaks
- gives greater privacy
- makes the day(s) different
- may be easier to raise personal issues

Off-site disadvantages:

- family care arrangements may be difficult
- unfamiliar journey
- unfamiliar building

- could be too daunting
- more expensive and difficult to organize than on-site
- encourages people who just want a day out

Privacy is the prime criterion, so cover up windows in doors, disconnect telephones and, to minimize disruptions, have messages left outside the course room.

Stand-alone or with other training?

The decision here is whether to run a stand-alone assertiveness course, promoted as such, or whether to include short sessions on assertiveness on other courses. This may be a strategic decision, influenced by wider training and human resource development objectives. Many organizations run both as a way of integrating assertiveness into the mainstream culture of the organization.

Assertiveness on its own

Advantages:

- makes the process clear
- allows practice in a safe environment on a range of situations
- enables people to concentrate fully on the ingredients and not be confused by other issues
- all participants come expecting to work on assertiveness
- concentrated practice increases effectiveness
- enables participants to see the wider applications
- increases the value attributed to it by the organization or individual
- enables assertiveness to be taught and practised in depth

Disadvantages:

- participants may not easily make the link to the application you may want or they may need
- they see it as a separate technique not a generic skill
- some people are reluctant to apply for an assertiveness course as they don't want to be seen to need it
- often people whose behaviour tends to aggression think they are already very assertive
- assertiveness has been confused with aggression in the past and managers may be reluctant to support it
- more likelihood of the 'course tornado' syndrome when someone rushes back to work and attempts to put everything into practice immediately!

Assertiveness as a part of other training

The appropriateness of this is entirely due to the nature of the host course, as it is important that the philosophy and approach of assertiveness does not clash with the wider subject and approach. However, assertiveness can enhance and deepen the subject and approach of many other courses. So it's important to do your homework before making the decision.

For example: be clear about the relationship between assertiveness and negotiation skills, sales techniques and anything including neurolinguistic programming. Mixing these together is likely to confuse participants and undermine the effectiveness of your training. However, including assertiveness with management skills, customer care training, stress management training, quality training or any wider communication skills training is likely to support and enhance the learning all round.

Assertiveness can be used in so many contexts.

As a communication skill it:

- can be used in many different aspects of communication: verbally, in day-to-day conversations, presentations, training, customer relations, negotiations, selling; in writing letters, memos, training and sales leaf-lets, electronic mail, proposals, and reports
- ensures that all parties state their position
- has a dynamic process rather than a series of inflexible steps
- places the responsibility for communication squarely with each individual
- gets away from repetitive techniques which can be ridiculed or become irritating
- promotes development rather than entrenchment in relationships
- makes true differences of opinion apparent and recognizable
- improves relationships between individuals and groups
- gives a set of ingredients which enhance inter-personal skills

As a life skill it:

- can be applied in work and personal lives
- leads to personal growth
- can become a way of life or life philosophy
- has all the advantages of the communication skills above
- is equally appropriate to women and men, old and young
- can span international differences when people realize cultural prefer-ences for particular aspects of assertiveness
- can work within families and personal relationships

As a transferable skill it:

- grows and develops with the individual, so assertiveness learned as a clerk can be transferred to management skills on promotion
- enhances other training, so a manager learning assertiveness as a per-sonal skill can also apply it to appraisal interviews and many other management situations
- bridges the gap between work and personal life, so assertiveness learned by a person at home with domestic responsibilities enhances their ability to build relationships when entering paid employment
- ensures that the organization gets good value for their investment

For example: on an in-depth five-day leadership course with senior managers, the poor quality of communication and feedback between the participants was slowing the course process down significantly. The trainer offered to run a short session on assertiveness which the participants welcomed and found to be immediately beneficial, not only on the course but also in most of the situations with which they were having difficulty back at work.

For example: sales people who were so deeply steeped in sales techniques were finding it difficult to build working relationships with non-sales staff. A two-day assertiveness workshop was an eye-opener to them and gave them an alternative process with which to behave.

Length of assertiveness courses or sessions

If there is unlimited time and scope available, the deciding factor will be the course objectives. However, as most trainers are working to very tight time constraints and with limited resources, it's more likely that the amount of time available has already been decided and your judgement is on what would be a realistic expected outcome in that time, for that particular group.

An introduction to assertiveness can take anything from a one-hour talk to a one-day workshop which will cover all the basics and give time for some practice. To cover assertiveness in any depth requires more than one day, and many stand-alone assertiveness courses last two or three days. There is little point in running assertiveness courses longer than this, as it is the practice which is most important and most difficult, so if more time is available, add follow-up days where progress can be assessed and built on, or make the training modular-based with one-day or half-day modules and time to practise in between.

The sample programmes which follow give examples of the amount of time needed to cover the content, and different ways of delivering the same content. They are for:

- a one-day workshop
- a two-day workshop
- four half-day modules
- a half-day follow-up

A session on assertiveness in a longer course could also be anything: a one-hour talk, a two-hour session or maybe even a whole day. The same programmes would apply and in addition it would be important to:

- build links and cross-refer to the subject matter of the host course
- stress that this is an *introduction* to assertiveness—it is not an in-depth session
- tell participants of any stand-alone assertiveness courses available and encourage them to enrol

One-day workshop

Objective
- to introduce assertiveness
- to ensure that participants understand what assertiveness is
- to enable participants to put the basic ingredients into practice

Session 1   Welcome—objectives—introductions
Session 2   Assertiveness
- what it is/isn't
- definition
- the five main ingredients
- why bother?

Session 3   Finding the assertive words
Group work on scenarios

Lunch

Session 4   Assertiveness in real situations
Small group work
Session 5   Additional skills
- listening
- body language

Session 6   Group work on real situations (repeat)
Session 7   (if time available)
Additional skills
- giving/receiving criticism
- saying 'No'

Session 8   Summary and action session

Two-day workshop

Objective   To give participants enough knowledge, understanding and experience in assertiveness to be more effective in their communications both at work and at home

Day 1   Session 1   Welcome—objectives—introductions
Session 2   Assertiveness: what it is and isn't
Definitions of aggressive, assertive and passive behaviour
Group discussions
Session 3   Assertiveness
- why it's difficult
- theories connected with it
- why bother with it?

Lunch

Session 4   How to do it
- the five basic ingredients in assertiveness
- work on scenarios in syndicates

Session 5   Work on real situations in small groups

	Session 6	The role and importance of words, tone of voice and body language Group exercises
	Session 7	Listening skills Group exercises
Day 2	Session 8	Review and recap
	Session 9	Additional techniques • saying 'No' • broken record
	Session 10	Work on real situations in small groups
	Lunch	
	Session 11	Additional techniques • giving criticism • giving and receiving compliments • giving and receiving feedback
	Session 12	Work on real situations in small groups
	Session 13	Summary and action session

Four half-day modules

Objective To ensure that participants have enough knowledge, understanding and experience in assertiveness to be able to practise it effectively in real situations

Module 1 Objectives of all four modules

Introductions

Assertiveness
• what it is and isn't
• definition
• why bother?
• the five main ingredients

Group work on scenarios

Action session

Module 2 Recap and review of progress

The importance of listening
• input
• exercises

Group work on real situations

Action session

Module 3 Recap and review of progress

The use of words, voice and appearance

Body language and body space
- input
- exercises

Group work on real situations

Action session

Module 4   Recap and review of progress

Input on whatever aspect with which participants are having the greatest difficulty, such as:
- giving and receiving criticism
- giving and receiving compliments
- saying 'No'
- dealing with aggression
- dealing with passivity
- being assertive with yourself

Group work on real situations

Summary

Action session

A half-day follow up

Objective
- to enable participants to assess their progress with assertiveness
- to enable participants to identify areas on which to work in the future
- to practise additional skills

Session 1   Welcome and objectives
Session 2   Progress review individually
- what's been going well?
- what's not been going well?

Session 3   Progress review in groups
Session 4   Recap main principles of assertiveness
Session 5   Input on additional skills such as using assertiveness when:
- you find inconsistency in someone's behaviour
- you need a response
- you aren't being listened to
- you're dealing with very strong feelings
- you have very strong feelings

if not already covered {
- you want to say 'no'
- you need to give/receive criticism
- you need to give/receive a compliment

Session 6   Group work on real situations
Session 7   Being assertive with yourself
Session 8   Summary and action session

Publicity about assertiveness

Publicity material about assertiveness courses is especially important as there is such widespread misunderstanding about the subject. For this reason, all the messages being sent out about assertiveness training, whether it be recruitment literature, reports, articles in the press, entries in course directories or word of mouth, need to be especially clear.

The difficulty of overcoming the misunderstandings, prejudices and assumptions which are made about assertiveness training lead some trainers to avoid using the word altogether. So in the past, assertiveness courses have been disguised under titles such as 'Communicating effectively', 'Dealing with difficult situations', 'Dealing with difficult people effectively', 'Getting your message across', and so on.

Avoiding the use of the word avoids assumptions and misunderstandings, but it also misleads potential participants. Many people might prefer that there were an alternative word, but the reality at the moment is that, if it is an assertiveness course, it is unassertive as well as misleading not to have the word 'assertiveness' prominent in the literature.

Janette Fiddaman in her case study of Littlewoods Home Shopping Division supports this view:

What do you call it? There was quite a lot of pressure to change the title in order to make the topic more acceptable. The advice I would give here is 'be assertive'. What is the point in introducing the concept of assertiveness training if you can't be confident enough to call it what it actually is.

Common views of assertiveness which are untrue are:

- aggression is assertive
- assertiveness is only for women
- assertiveness is only for people who can't stand up for themselves
- only people who have problems need assertiveness
- assertiveness is about tricking people
- assertiveness is about always getting your own way

These common perceptions can dissuade those people using passive behaviour from attending because they do not want to become overbearing bullies, and also put off those people who use aggressive behaviour because they already believe themselves to be assertive! They can also dissuade those who would like to learn *assertiveness* because they believe the course will be about *aggression*.

Jane Beck, who runs assertiveness courses inside organizations, illustrates these subjective views in her case study:

The response by organisations to the word 'assertiveness' shows a widespread misunderstanding of it. In one organisation where I trained both sexes the women were told 'Oh! so you're going to learn to be aggressive!' The message to men in the same company was 'Ah! I hear you're going on the wimps course!'

These commonly held views mean that assertiveness training is often controversial—everyone has a view on what assertiveness is and who it's for. This controversy and these mistaken ideas about assertiveness have to be challenged head on in all pre- and post-course material.

Important content in publicity material is:

- the definition of assertiveness
- comparisons with passive and (especially) aggressive behaviour with examples
- emphasis that assertiveness is a *behaviour*, not a personality trait
- emphasis that assertiveness can be learnt
- lots of examples of situations where assertiveness would be useful for this particular target group
- course content
- reasonable expectations from the course
- self-nomination and what this means

The most powerful publicity medium for training is word of mouth, so the most effective publicity will be through past participants as word gets around the organization.

For example: an assertiveness course in a large retail organization which was specifically introduced to help people from disadvantaged groups had to be relaunched after the first six months of running as the course had established such a positive following in the organization that mainstream managers had taken it over for themselves! Annoying for the training department, but a compliment to the effectiveness of the training.

Not only will potential participants not enrol because they have a false impression of assertiveness, but they will also have barriers placed in their way by other staff. Running the gauntlet of aggressive remarks such as 'You don't need an assertiveness course, you're assertive (meaning aggressive) enough already!' and jokes may strengthen their resolve to attend or put them off.

On their return after the course, participants may also have to deal with derogatory comments, often disguised as a joke, such as:

> 'Go on then—do it!'
> 'Is that it then—is that assertiveness?'
> 'Look out everybody, Sam is going to be assertive now!'
> Hoots of derisive laughter at an attempt at assertiveness

Sometimes participants will choose to work on these re-entry situations whilst on the course, as these can be particularly painful tests of their determination and unpractised skills.

Other additional hurdles to be faced by a potential participant are identified in Chapter 2.

The trainer as role model

In addition to the ground rules outlined in Chapter 5, an additional ground rule when running assertiveness courses is that the trainer becomes the role model in a more powerful and immediate way than in other forms of training. This is because assertiveness training is about a form of behaviour, so it can be demonstrated, or not demonstrated, all the time, in whatever situation. The trainer's credibility, therefore, is more tested and vulnerable on assertiveness courses than on many others. Equally, the effect of a positive role model may be the most powerful influence on the participants.

Part of the process of learning requires taking risks and experimenting. Participants will only be able to do this if they feel respect for and trust the trainer. This respect and trust can be built by trainers who are visibly practising what they preach.

Being a good role model means:

- actively working on your own assertiveness
- sharing your own experiences of successes and failures with assertiveness
- practising assertiveness whilst running the course with everyone; participants, speakers, caterers, administrators, etc.
- admitting when you don't know the answer

In addition, if trainers are in-house, participants may already know them as colleagues, socially, on other courses, as bosses, or as subordinates. In this case, trainers are especially under the microscope as role models, as participants will be able to compare the trainer's behaviour inside the course room to that which they see used outside.

Case studies

In the case studies that follow, five past participants of courses describe their experience of having attended assertiveness courses, and ways in which they have subsequently found assertiveness helpful. The case studies are written in their own words, with an introductory paragraph from us.

Case study

> **Pete Hodgson demonstrates how the application of assertiveness skills has improved the effectiveness of his relationships with colleagues and customers.**

Pete Hodgson,
BT

I nominated myself for the assertiveness training course. I'd heard a lot about the programme and I was confident the training would help me improve my overall effectiveness at work.

A high proportion of my time is spent in meetings with customers and colleagues and I have found that effective communication skills are essential if projects are to run smoothly and successfully. My role as project manager means that I have overall responsibility for the success of projects but I am increasingly aware of the dependence I have on the positive cooperation of all those involved. The main difficulty I face in these circumstances is maintaining the commitment of project team members with no direct line management control over their activities.

Clear contracts at the beginning of the projects are an essential ingredient in the process, but things rarely go according to plan and I was looking for assertiveness skills to help me in these situations. For example, I recently took over responsibility for a training programme for internal trainers. The programme was transferred from another group who had developed the material. They were not happy about transferring the work to a group who, in their view, were not competent to manage the programme effectively. In order to achieve a successful handover it was important that we had a constructive relationship, but I was angry with their attitude and responded aggressively. The result was an almost complete breakdown in the relationship resulting in serious delays in the delivery programme. During the assertiveness training I reflected on this and similar experiences and focused on techniques for defusing potential conflict by recognizing my own feelings and respecting those of others.

One of the most important features of the assertiveness training for me was the technique of 'disclosure'. This is the process of disclosing how you feel before you say what you want. It sounds simple, but it is amazing the number of times I have used it to great effect since the training course.

Of course, it's no good just dumping your feelings on others. A major aspect of behaving assertively is standing up for your own 'rights' but not in a manner which denies others theirs. Simply defining assertiveness in this manner helped me to differentiate between assertive and aggressive behaviour. I found this to be particularly important because it challenged long-held beliefs that to act aggressively (e.g. by intimidating others) was to behave assertively. The aspect of the training which surprised me the most was how difficult it was to say 'no'. I have practised many of the techniques from the course but I struggle with this one more than any other. Sometimes I am inclined to justify my views at length and complicate things unnecessarily rather than just say 'no'. Of course this can have serious consequences as it distorts the process of communication between people and muddies the water. People can easily leave meetings with confused or distorted views simply due to the fear of using the 'N' word.

More recently I experience much greater levels of cooperation and support in the teams I project manage, and the relationship I have with internal customers. There tends to be a greater degree of clarity and fewer, less damaging periods of conflict. I often find that problems and disagreements, which previously caused so much disharmony, are resolved more quickly.

As a result of the training, I feel that I behave more assertively at work and at home. My family would probably tell you that I lose my temper a little less often than I used to, but I doubt anyone would suggest I had undergone a personality change. Nevertheless, I will always regard the assertiveness training course as one of the most beneficial training programmes I have experienced.

Case Study

> **Stella Wiseman outlines clearly the benefits of assertiveness in terms of increases in self-esteem and confidence. However, she issues a timely warning about the dangers of opening up old wounds during intensive assertiveness courses and running the risk that there is neither the time nor the expertise to resolve the issues before the course ends. (This case study appeared first as 'Two steps forward, one step back' in the February 1994 issue of *Everywoman* magazine, and is reproduced here with their kind permission.)**

Stella Wiseman   I am shy. I don't like telephoning people I don't know. But telephones became a necessary part of a new job. A possible solution came to mind: an assertiveness course.

I had long considered doing such a course. They seemed to have some magical power. I had watched two friends transform themselves under this power from, if not timid then certainly unconfident people, to dynamic women who got things done. One found a good job after months of searching, the other dealt successfully with a work placement as a probation officer in a men's prison. If they could do it, so could I, but it still took me several years to get round to it.

Finally I signed up for an intensive three-day assertiveness course for women, run at an adult education centre. With me were others of different ages and backgrounds. At the start of the course we were told that attending was an assertive thing to do. It was certainly a commitment, since most of us had busy lives, and we soon discovered that it was also a luxury: three days of thinking about ourselves and not worrying about other people.

Why, we were asked, were we there? The answers were surprisingly varied. I had assumed that most people would come because they were shy. However, a frightening number announced calmly that they were too aggressive and wanted to learn how to act assertively instead. I fervently hoped that I wouldn't have to get into a small discussion group with one of these. Within minutes I was in just such a group, with just such a woman, discussing what we hoped to achieve from the course. 'I want to learn how to listen better,' she said. It soon became clear that there is little difference between a shy or passive person and an aggressive one; both suffer from low self-esteem.

Self-esteem and behaviour are closely linked. Other people form opinions about us based on what we do and how, and this determines how they behave to us. This reinforces our level of self-esteem which influences our behaviour, and so on. Our own low self-esteem leads others to treat us with little respect, while high self-esteem has the opposite effect. Of course we are entitled to equal respect whatever our level of self-esteem, but since we rarely receive this it is up to us to change things.

Over the next three days we learned how. Basic to assertiveness training is the need to acquire certain skills such as saying 'no', or making requests clearly without being deflected. Behind all this is the belief that we have the right to act in this way—though acquiring this belief is generally far harder than learning the skills.

Some of this was remarkably straightforward. We found that simply straightening our backs, breathing from our diaphragms and holding our heads up made a difference to the way we projected ourselves. Other skills, such as making requests, were harder to learn—often because they touched on deep-seated problems, years of saying 'yes' instead of 'no': long years, in fact, of not treating ourselves as important. Some of the exercises brought unexpected hurts to the surface.

This demonstrates a potentially serious problem with assertiveness training, particularly on intensive courses. Before starting mine I was warned by a psychiatrist friend to take care. She had recently come across a young woman who had had a breakdown following a management course which involved assertiveness training. It had unearthed some serious emotional problems but had not offered her the means of dealing with them. At the time I didn't take my friend's warning seriously, but by the end of the course I could see her point. While some of us were elated by exercises such as 'throwing away' criticism, others felt profoundly disturbed or vulnerable. At least one woman was in tears.

Issues such as dealing with criticism or combating a negative self-image, which may stem from childhood experiences, can rarely be solved in a few hours within a group of people who hardly know each other. Assertiveness training should not take the place of counselling.

Overall, however, does it work? One woman I telephoned a few months later told me: 'I think it's made a difference. I know more what I want and I am more prepared to ask for it. I'm still working on my self-esteem but I feel less hemmed in by my inadequacies, more prepared to take risks. I have always had problems projecting my voice because I've felt I have nothing worth saying, but at work recently someone commented that I sounded confident and assertive. They even asked me if I'd been on an assertiveness course, so I suppose it must have helped.'

Ringing her was encouraging. It reminded me of the way I had felt at the end of the course: that change was possible, that I had the right to look after myself and make demands. The problem is that it's easy to forget that. Assertiveness courses are not magic spells, but part of a long-term commitment to ourselves. Learning to be assertive requires hard work and the support of other people. But if it means I can pick up the telephone and ask for something, then I'm on my way.

Case study

> **The most positive aspects of assertiveness training for Alison Hustwitt were firstly discovering that it wasn't 'aggression' in disguise and secondly learning to say 'no'. Alison's application of assertiveness has benefited her life outside work as much as inside.**

Alison Hustwitt,
Gloucester City
Volunteer Bureau

I came to assertiveness having just survived the worst year of my life; my younger brother had died of cancer, my mother was recovering from lung cancer, I was made redundant and my marriage had broken up after appalling behaviour on my husband's part. Having negotiated my way through this, and retained my sanity, I was already a stronger, more confident person than hitherto.

What assertiveness did for me was to make me aware of certain patterns and negatives. I was expecting it to be along the lines of the 'gung ho' American examples which I had read about—rather loud and aggressive—so I was a little apprehensive. It was a pleasant surprise therefore to find the course was in fact designed to promote polite, firm but non-confrontational assertiveness.

I recognized that for me non-assertive behaviour had included always coping—no matter how unfair or outrageous life, or other people, seemed, I prided myself on my ability to cope, complete the task, shoulder the burden. I wasn't a total 'flossie' (a person who thinks promotion comes from working hard and being indispensable) because I didn't do everything uncomplainingly or invisibly, but I was over-stretched, stressed and not as effective as I could have been. Realizing that I did not have to cover every gap, take on every crisis, mediate every dispute, that I could simply say 'no' was a great moment. I realized further that I tend to qualify and amplify what I saw, even in circumstances where it becomes long-winded or an opening for people to contest what should have been a straightforward 'no'.

I was able during the course, with the help of a small group, to identify the conflicting messages which I was conveying to my former husband, because my body language and defensive stance were carrying the opposite message to my actual words. I found the role playing to share or solve problems very helpful, and working with the other women and seeing some of them grow in confidence was a rewarding aspect of the course.

I work in a voluntary organization staffed mainly by cooperative assertive women and although the training has once or twice been useful when dealing with our management committee, and officialdom in general, its main value has been in improving my confidence for public speaking and outreach work. In the rest of my life it has been very helpful in allowing me to say 'no', or to place limits on my time; I have felt more in control when chairing meetings or negotiating with various groups.

It was an added bonus that for the first time in my life I politely, but firmly, shut the door on Jehovah's Witnesses and have been similarly firm with other unwanted doorstep or telephone callers.

The trainer's own example of courteous, firm assertive behaviour was one of the most helpful things about the course. Learning how to deal with situations or people who in the past would have reduced me to inarticulate rage, or worse, tears, was made easier by her example. I am now able to reason more effectively and logically, even when listening to conflicting or infuriating arguments.

So much has changed in my life so rapidly that putting the effects of assertiveness training in context isn't easy. I do feel that it has underpinned the growth and change in my life, given me improved confidence in my ability to deal with people, enabled me to express myself in a more logical way, and in doing all of the above considerably reduced my susceptibility to stress.

Case study

> **Simon Templar used attendance at an assertiveness course as an opportunity to review his management style, tone down indirect aggression and put himself in the other person's shoes. Feedback in his work situations shows it's working.**

Simon Templar,
BT

Before attending the course I had a misconception that assertiveness and an aggressive management style went hand in hand. This was reinforced by the management style operating in the workplace at that particular time. My own management style before going on the event was more or less a *laissez-faire* approach and a policy of trying to avoid conflict in the workplace by negotiating a win/win outcome, often resulting in myself giving ground to ensure an outcome. Initial feeling on being nominated for the course was that assertiveness would mean adopting a style of management which was alien to my nature.

With regard to my management style after the course, I felt that my own style was appropriate for me, although better knowledge of and the application of situation management, reinforced by the assertiveness techniques learned on the course, would improve my own management style. The myth that assertiveness management style equals an aggressive style was removed.

When people are first appointed to a management position and are getting to grips with the job in hand, the skill of managing people or situations tends to take second place to the actual job. Thus feedback from peers tends to be as follows:

- be more assertive
- contribute more to meetings
- tell them, don't ask them, to do a piece of work

The course changed my attitude to people management in two fundamental ways:

- sarcasm is the use of indirect aggression and is very destructive to a working relationship and can hurt people's feelings
- I try to put myself in the position of the other person before making a decision, to decide which management style would be appropriate for that individual or situation.

The most important aspect of the training for me was the use of role plays and group discussion which illustrated the different styles of management; also the opportunity of seeing the effect of using the wrong style and the consequences of getting it wrong in a safe environment. The interactive video package which fronted the course was a very helpful introduction to the tools and techniques of assertiveness.

The environment created by the tutors enabled the delegates to talk in an open and honest way, which enabled the team to learn by people's own experiences.

One example where assertiveness training has improved my own style is better use of delegation, and improving my confidence to make a contribution to group meetings.

The hardest area of assertiveness is the use of assertive language, for example when you are a child you are told that it is wrong to use 'I want' but 'may I have' is acceptable. In my opinion you become conditioned to not using assertive language at an early age, thus making it difficult to change your outlook.

Feedback from my peers has been very positive, and this has been reinforced by my own perception. The knowledge gained from the course has improved my confidence to use my own management style and question others.

Case study

> **Being accused of being aggressive was a never-to-be-forgotten experience for Lorraine Chimes. Assertiveness, she thought, was making her views heard and getting her own way. Two days of assertiveness training changed her view and gave her the opportunity to build better relationships at home and at work.**

Lorraine Chimes,
Barking and Dagenham
Council for Voluntary
Service

I have lots of friends and members of my family who like to get their own way: I sometimes do too!

My perception of assertiveness before the course was using my aggression to get my own way; the trouble was I wasn't the most liked person in the office or at home and although I got my way I didn't feel too good about it, and whenever I wanted to be assertive by saying 'no' I always seemed to bring an aggressive attitude in. When I think back, I must have acted very rudely towards my colleagues at work. I remember my Dad saying to me once 'If only your sister were more aggressive like you, people wouldn't walk all over her.'

Since attending a two-day workshop on assertiveness with Jean Buswell (Gloucestershire and West of England Training Initiative) my whole attitude has changed, and at the same time others' attitudes have changed towards me.

I have a better relationship with my children and my husband, my friends and work colleagues—I only wish they could go on the course too!

I think that choosing my words more carefully and my use of body language have changed the way I react to asking and refusing. Instead of either losing my temper or swallowing my feelings I have managed to achieve the right way to ask or refuse. I enjoyed the course so much that I was really sad that it had to come to an end. Jean Buswell was a very professional trainer who made us all (a group of eight women) feel completely at ease with each other within minutes. There were lots of handouts; I still look back at mine so that I don't slip back into my old ways.

I think some of the participants found the role play quite difficult, but being able to say no does take some practice.

Parent—adult—child
(a reference to
transactional analysis)

I found that I was usually either in the free child mode or the nurturing parent mode. One of my daughters was usually in the critical parent mode.

When I came home after the first day on the course, my daughter was doing her homework. I asked her if I could play the new tape which I had just bought; she said no at first, and then said 'OK, but only once— I'm trying to concentrate'. I realized after about ten minutes that we should probably be reversing our roles: doesn't the child usually want to play the music and the parent say 'no'? Since this incident I tend to react differently towards my daughter, and I think we would probably be at each others' throats by now if I hadn't attended the assertiveness training, because she is 16 and I am going on 17!

I really do congratulate Jean Buswell for her professionalism in the way the course was conducted and for helping me to become someone who is nice to know.

Summary

This chapter has built on the general points made in Chapter 5 by outlining further aspects of training which are of particular importance when running assertiveness courses. The key points raised are:

- choices about venue, target group, length of session and whether it is stand-alone or part of a longer course will strongly influence the effectiveness of the training
- assertiveness has a strong contribution to make to many other subjects
- everyone has a view on assertiveness—often mistaken—and this has to be tackled in course publicity materials
- to run effective assertiveness courses, trainers have to be practising assertiveness themselves
- people respond to assertiveness very personally
- assertiveness training can be personally challenging—for the trainer as well as the participants

References

Research results *'Women-only Training'* by Liz Willis and Jenny Daisley, The Springboard Consultancy, (forthcoming).

Wiseman, Stella (1994) 'Two steps forward, one step back', *Everywoman*, February issue.

Working with Men, July 1991.

7 Assertiveness in evaluation

This chapter looks at the role of assertiveness in evaluation before, during and after the training. In particular it considers:

- why assertiveness is important in evaluation
- who evaluates training
- applying the five ingredients of assertiveness to evaluation
- trainers receiving feedback assertively
- using assertive questions and questionnaires in evaluation

The case for evaluation in general and explanation of the mechanics of it are to be found in Bramley (1990). Specific pointers on the evaluation of women-only training are to be found in Willis and Daisley (1992).

Why assertiveness is important in evaluation

Measuring the results in terms of benefits to the organization and to the individual is crucial to the success of any piece of training. Organizations need to know that their resources are being used effectively and that the training is meeting the needs which it identified in the first place. For individuals, being conscious of their new knowledge, attitude or skill enhances their learning. If the evaluation process does not elicit accurate and true information, it is worthless.

Evaluation takes place against the objectives that have been set for the training, and it is best if the evaluation strategy and methods are set up at the same time as setting the objectives so that pre-course as well as post-course evaluation information can be considered.

Assertiveness is, therefore, crucial in the collection of evaluation information because:

- it improves the quality of the information gathered
- evaluation costs time and money
- collecting inaccurate information wastes time and money
- you cannot assume that participants and their managers always tell you the truth
- participants tending to passivity need to be drawn out
- participants tending to aggression need to have their messages heard
- as a trainer you need to be able to receive and deal with positive and negative feedback assertively

Who evaluates training?

Assertive trainers seek feedback on their work so that it can be developed, updated, fine tuned and improved. In some instances the trainers who have run the course also carry out the evaluation. This has the advantages that they:

- are very familiar with the material
- know the objectives set
- are aware of all other factors which influenced that particular course, such as poor accommodation, a particularly difficult participant, several false fire alarms during the course, and so on
- are aware of the variety of results that may be possible with this training

On the other hand the disadvantages of the trainers who have run the course also conducting the evaluation are that they:

- have a vested interest in the results
- may not always be open to negative feedback
- may be affected by having had very good or very bad relationships with the participants

Where the person evaluating the training is not the trainer who designed or ran the course it is important to ensure that:

- there is a full briefing about the course, its objectives, content, methods and philosophy
- objectivity is maintained and that the evaluator has no personal stake in the results
- there is full cooperation between trainer and evaluator

For example: when designing the Springboard Women's Development Programme (Willis and Daisley, 1994) we consciously decided that it was important to include small-group work which was not facilitated. This decision had to be clearly communicated to the person carrying out evaluation studies in one organization where facilitators abounded in training and in meetings generally, as there was likely to be a strong reaction to groups without a facilitator.

For example: a trainer reported having to speak up assertively when another trainer was appointed to evaluate a personal development programme as the appointed trainer had previously been an opponent of the personal development programme, favouring the career development programme she'd designed herself instead.

Whoever evaluates the training, they need to be skilled in training, questionnaire design and interviewing, all of which are influenced by assertiveness.

The evaluator can use assertiveness in evaluation interviews to:

- draw out accurate feelings as well as thoughts and results
- be totally objective and impersonal with the participant even if strong feelings are being expressed

● establish joint solutions

Unassertive interviewers can leave out part of the picture if the feedback is difficult for them to receive. This may be because they are personally offended or upset by the participants' strong negative feelings about the course, or because they are dismissive or simply do not hear positive reactions.

Applying the five ingredients to evaluation

Whether the evaluation is conducted by questionnaire or by interview, the five key ingredients of assertiveness can influence the process. All five need to be used in one form or another to make the results as accurate and reliable as possible. In addition, applying the ingredients enables the participant to continue the process of learning. This is especially applicable in an interview. Consider the relevance of each ingredient.

Listen The whole purpose of evaluation is to listen to what everyone concerned with the training programme has to say about it. These people may be:

- **participants** listen to what they say about the training, its content and process, the results back at work, the trainers and their performance and the administration
- **participants' managers** listen to what they say about what their expectations were of the course, why they agreed to that member of staff attending it, what changes they have perceived back at work, what conversations they have had with the participant before, during and after the training and what action (if any) they have taken to support the learning after the training
- **other colleagues whose work is affected by the participant's work** this will mean creatively discovering who has day-to-day contact. It may include peer groups and other departments. For example, in a public relations company, 'management control' workshops revealed that there was a substantial need for account directors to have better information about detailed accounts and billing timescales so they could produce billing information more quickly and had speedier knowledge of 'overservicing' (spending more hours than budgeted). In this case, a key supplier of evaluation information after the workshop was the billing clerk in the accounts department who was questioned to discover whether the account directors (who are many grades higher) were producing billing information more quickly and accurately than before
- **suppliers and customers** both have key information related to the performance of people inside the organization and can be included in evaluation. The ideas of lean production described in Chapter 2 indicate that organizations need to build substantially better relationships with the complete chain of activity around their businesses. Surveys

of customers and their perception of the organization need to take account of recent training. Equally important is the impact of training on relationships with suppliers

Top quality listening in evaluation means:

- remaining open to what people have to say, even if it is unpalatable
- listening to people's thoughts, feelings and intentions, to get the fullest picture of the effect of the course
- finding the balance between allowing people to say all that they have to say and letting them ramble on unchecked
- keeping interruptions to a minimum
- being able to demonstrate that you have listened and understood

Demonstrate that you understand

As explained in Chapter 2, demonstrating that you understand means much more than just *saying* that you understand. Before conducting the evaluation the person conducting it needs to really understand what the training is about and what it is capable of achieving. **For example**: there is no point in asking participants whether the trainer gave enough advice and support after a course, if the course had been specifically designed to promote self-reliance and independence from the trainer.

The evaluation itself also needs to be reflected back and summarized to the participants so that they know that they have been heard and understood. This is particularly true of evaluation interviews where the objectivity of the interviewer is paramount and participants may be anxious about whether their views are being accurately represented.

Say what you think and feel

While it's important for evaluators to be able to say what they think and feel about what is being conveyed to them, the most effective use of this ingredient in evaluation is in the evaluators' ability to encourage the participants to say what they really think and feel. This can be difficult as people do not always know what it is that they think and feel about an experience and they are not always used to expressing it. The evaluator can help:

- by very clear and specific questioning
- by giving options which include thoughts and feelings that may not have been thought of
- by probing further in evaluation interviews

Because this process is so important, end-of-course discussions are not recommended as participants with very strong views can overwhelm the others or prevent their voices being heard. As most good training aims to send participants away feeling positive, starting evaluation discussions just before they leave gives a mixed message and may undermine the training if some participants hadn't liked a particular exercise, the venue or the lunch! Also, it may be that at the time, the new learning (particularly about themselves and their attitudes) was not a comfortable process and requires some digestion and practice before the person is able to look positively on the experience. If course participants have been given challenging feedback they will need time to accept and assimilate it, however constructively the feedback has been given.

Anonymous evaluation questionnaires can help to ensure that thoughts and feelings are collected from people who may otherwise be shy of expressing them and having them attributed.

Say what you want to happen In addition to questions about the course itself, evaluation questions also need to facilitate participants' views on what needs to happen next. For example:

- follow-up training
- further action by themselves
- action by their managers
- action by the training department

In addition, the evaluator's views also need to be expressed on what they consider should happen next, as, by conducting the evaluation, they will have had a unique overview of the course, the participants, any other interviewees and the overall strengths and vulnerabilities of the training.

Consider the consequences of joint solutions This is applicable where, through the evaluation, participants make suggestions for improvement. In this case the evaluator needs to explore the relevance, applicability and consequences of the suggestions made without dismissing them. There also needs to be some feedback to the participants about their suggestions and about the consequences of them being used or discarded. **For example**: a trainer had difficulty with one group on a course who strongly questioned why a particular exercise was being used when they knew of previous participants who recommended that it should be changed. A full discussion of the consequences of the change needed to have taken place with the previous participants for everyone to understand why the exercise had been retained.

The most effective application of the five ingredients of assertiveness to evaluation will result in:

- the evaluator doing more listening than talking
- the evaluator demonstrating understanding
- the participants' thoughts and feelings being predominant in conversations, but not to the exclusion of those of the evaluator
- both evaluator and participants expressing what they want to happen
- an equal discussion taking place about the consequences of joint solutions

Trainers receiving feedback

An important way of improving and developing training is through feedback. Feedback through evaluation may be about:

- **the content of the course** in relation to the needs of the individuals and the organization. It's usually easier to take negative feedback if you didn't design the course yourself. If you did design the course yourself then a special effort is needed to remain objective when receiving negative feedback
- **the course process and methods** in relation to the content, type and level of people and the current situation in the organization
- **the performance and behaviour of the trainer** and its appropriateness to the content and the participants

If you have identified the training needs, designed and developed and then delivered the programme yourself, then *all* the feedback is immediately relevant to you and it is especially important to be able to separate out feedback that is personal to you from general feedback about the course.

The assertive guidelines that follow were outlined in Chapter 5, and will help you extract feedback that is constructive rather than destructive.

Remain open and listen

All trainers can be touched personally by feedback at some time in their careers. It may be the positive reading of evaluation forms that say:

- how wonderful you were
- how you changed someone's life for the better
- how well you organized the course
- how sensitive you were to individual needs
- how good your design and content were

On the other hand it may be feedback that initially seems negative or challenging such as:

- very personal negative feedback about your behaviour
- personality traits that people didn't like
- your lack of professionalism
- mistakes in course design
- a mistake you made in running the course
- the clothes you wear or the type of car you drive

Trainers need to be tough enough to be able to really listen and take in what people are saying about them without dismissing it. This means understanding the feedback before any conclusions are made about what it is that has been said and what action, if any, might be taken. One of the key learning points in receiving feedback is to remain open to the negative parts but to really take in all the positive messages as well. This means paying particular attention to the facts and seeing the full range of the feedback. Most people assume that positive feedback is easy to assimilate, but that isn't always so. Trainers often pore over evaluation forms and note only the negatives whilst ignoring the positives.

For example: an evaluation asked the participants to rate the course on a scale of 1 to 7 (1 being 'of no use' and 7 being 'of substantial use'). All the replies were in the 5–7 category, and 75 per cent of them scored the course as 6 or 7. In addition, the actions taken by participants following the course indicated that they were putting the material learned into practice. The personal feedback for the trainers was that they had shown a high degree of professionalism and the word 'excellent' was often used about them. However, in the space for general comments, two participants had commented that they felt that one trainer had been over-enthusiastic and too authoritarian. For this trainer, who had never before had feedback about being over-enthusiastic and authoritarian, despite most of the messages being positive, this was the only one which really struck home.

Listening to the participants' feelings is also important. People do not always state their feelings clearly, so you may have to clarify their feelings with them. Listen to your own feelings too, and express and acknowledge them to the people giving you feedback. Feelings may sometimes take a few days to emerge, so if you need time to realize what you are feeling, give yourself that time.

Ask questions to clarify your understanding

To clarify that you really understand the feedback you may need specific information and ideas about what the participants want you to do about it, particularly when feedback is vague or general. This does not mean that you will necessarily comply!

For example: if you are told that the pace of the day was too slow, ask:

- was there too little material in the day?
- did you pause too much between ideas?
- did you speak too slowly?
- was time taken up by other participants clarifying points, and this slowed things down?
- was too much time allocated for lunch and refreshment breaks?
- was the day too long?

Specific information is needed so that decisions can be made later whether or not to take action. Once there is clear understanding about what is meant by both positive and negative feedback, move on to the next stage.

Decide and communicate your decision

If, at this stage, you agree with all or part of the feedback and are prepared to take action, then say so. If, on the other hand, you are not sure or want time to think, indicate when you will respond. Take a reasonable time to respond and decide:

- is it all true?
- is it partly true?
- is it all false?
- what do you want to do about it?

Then if you are face to face with the person tell them your decision—assertively, of course!

Most evaluation feedback is by questionnaire and so participants often get no feedback that their comments have been received, understood and may or may not be acted upon. Consider:

- publishing a summary of the evaluation and state the actions which will be taken
- where questionnaires are not anonymous giving a response directly to the person(s) who made suggestions for change
- if a follow-up session is held, giving responses and feedback then

Change your behaviour or your course only if you want to

Only you can decide whether or not you are prepared to attempt a behaviour change. There may of course be pressure, sometimes irresistible, from your client or your boss who may wish to impose changes. Be assertive! Changing may depend on how easy or difficult this will be for you and how motivated you are to change. Inexperienced trainers sometimes rush too easily into assuming they were wrong and change perfectly good training because one small group had felt uncomfortable. Equally, very experienced trainers need to make sure that they are still open to change and have not slid into complacency.

Using assertive questions and questionnaires in evaluation

Good questions elicit good answers, and assertive questions are more likely to obtain assertive responses than passive and aggressive questions. In traditional question technique for interviews or questionnaires, it is taught that open questions beginning with 'who?', 'what?', 'where?', 'why?', 'when?' and 'how?' will give the best answers, and closed questions that give a 'yes' or 'no' answer should be used sparingly and only when no further amplification is necessary.

Leading questions are to be avoided because they manipulate people into answers which they might not think of for themselves. For example: 'How well did the trainer do?' . . . is leading, but 'What did the trainer do well?' coupled with 'What could the trainer have done better?' is more likely to get a more accurate response.

Assertive questions:

- are clear
- are specific
- don't make assumptions
- recognize the possibility of a wide range of answers
- demonstrate respect for the trainer and the participants

- encourage assertive answers
- are non-judgemental
- indicate the amount and type of detail needed in reply

Consider: 'What did you think of the programme?' This is very general and could result in one-word answers—'Great!' or 'Dreadful'—or six pages with comments about the lunches and teas, the course content, the venue, the other participants and the trainer.

Alternatively: 'Which sessions benefited you most and why?', and 'Which session benefited you least and why?' used together, focus the respondent's mind on to a specific aspect whilst still leaving open the possibility of a wide range of answers.

The more specific your need for information the more specific the questions will need to be. These are a few examples of questions which can be used in post-course questionnaires.

How did you find the pace of the programme overall?

too slow	☐
about right	☐
too fast	☐

How do you rate the course overall?

of great help	☐
of considerable help	☐
of some help	☐
not much help at all	☐
no use whatsoever	☐

How did you hear about the programme?

from my line manager	☐
from my personnel manager	☐
by letter	☐
from a poster	☐
from my training officer	☐
from a colleague	☐
on my pay-slip	☐
from a mentor	☐
other (please state)	☐

If questions like these are used in interviews then the assertive way to record them is to have the options written on card or paper so that the participant can see the evaluator indicating the number or letter of the reply.

To obtain the best possible results, pre-course questionnaires can also be used. On pp. 139–141 Fig. 7.1 (reproduced with kind permission from the Women's Unit at The Department of Health) shows the use of spectra which give respondents even greater flexibility and subtlety of response.

The same form, with additional questions about post-course results, was issued three months after the end of the course, enabling a direct comparison to be made of the changes in feelings and behaviour before and after the training. In addition, similar forms were sent to the participants' managers to obtain an alternative view of changes.

Summary

Questionnaire design and question technique will always be enhanced by the application of assertiveness. Questions will be crisper and more specific, and achieve the intended result. Feedback will be solicited and received more effectively by the trainer, and will be more likely to lead to further action.

References

Bramley, Peter (1990) *Evaluating the Effectiveness of Training*, McGraw-Hill, Maidenhead.

Willis, Liz and Daisley, Jenny (1992) *Developing Women through Training*, McGraw-Hill, Maidenhead.

Willis, Liz and Daisley, Jenny (1994) *Springboard Womens' Development Workbook*, 3rd edition, Hawthorn Press, Stroud.

Name: _____

Contact address: _____

_____

_____

Job title: _____

Please circle the number which is closest to your usual behaviour.

Confidence

1. How confident are you:

    (a) At work:

1	2	3	4	5	6	7	8

    never   always

    (b) At home:

1	2	3	4	5	6	7	8

    never   always

How others see you

2. Are you surprised by the way other people react to things you say or do:

    (a) At work:

1	2	3	4	5	6	7	8

    never   always

    (b) At home:

1	2	3	4	5	6	7	8

    never

    always

Voicing your opinion

3. How often do you express your views:

    (a) At work in meetings of three or more people:

1	2	3	4	5	6	7	8

    never   always

(b) At work in one-to-one meetings:

| 1 | 2 | 3 | 4 | 5 | 6 | 7 | 8 |

never   always

(c) At home:

| 1 | 2 | 3 | 4 | 5 | 6 | 7 | 8 |

never   always

Self-development

4. Do you feel that you are 'making the best' of yourself:

(a) At work:

| 1 | 2 | 3 | 4 | 5 | 6 | 7 | 8 |

no   always

(b) At home:

| 1 | 2 | 3 | 4 | 5 | 6 | 7 | 8 |

no   always

What (if anything) do you think is holding you back

(c) at work: _____

_____

(d) at home: _____

_____

Falling in with others' plans

5. Do you find yourself doing things that you really do not want to do but have never said so:

(a) At work:

| 1 | 2 | 3 | 4 | 5 | 6 | 7 | 8 |

never   always

(b) At home:

| 1 | 2 | 3 | 4 | 5 | 6 | 7 | 8 |

never   always

Control

6. How much control do you feel you have over events which affect you:

(a) At work:

```
1       2       3       4       5       6       7       8
|-------|-------|-------|-------|-------|-------|-------|
never                                               always
```

(b) At home:

```
1       2       3       4       5       6       7       8
|-------|-------|-------|-------|-------|-------|-------|
never                                               always
```

Objectives

7. Please list a few of the things you would like to get out of this course:

_____

_____

_____

_____

_____

_____

_____

_____

_____

_____

_____

_____

_____

_____

Thank you for taking the time to complete this questionnaire

Please check that you have entered your personal details on the front page of this questionnaire and then return it to:

_____

Figure 7.1   *Pre-course self-assessment questionnaire*

Appendix

This appendix contains useful information for the further study of
assertiveness and sample material for assertiveness courses:

- useful books
- sources of material for use on assertiveness courses
- training assertiveness trainers
- sample handouts for assertiveness courses

Useful books

Ken and Kate Back (1990) *Assertiveness at Work*, McGraw-Hill,
Maidenhead.
Considered by many to be the definitive book on assertiveness at work.
Good background reading. Recently updated.

Eric Berne (1964) *Games People Play*, Penguin, London.
A classic book which moves Transactional Analysis from academic
theory into everyday situations.

Anne Dickson (1994) *A Woman in your Own Right*, Quartet, London.
Highly regarded guide to assertiveness with emphasis on techniques.
Written for women but also of relevance to men.

Beverley Hare (1988) *Be Assertive*, Optima, London.
Good introduction.

Thomas Harris (1970) *I'm OK, You're OK*, Pan, London.
The best-selling and frequently reprinted introduction to Transactional
Analysis.

Amy and Thomas Harris (1986) *Staying OK*, Pan, London.
The follow-up to *I'm OK, You're OK*.

Allan Pease (1981) *Body Language*, Sheldon Press, London.
Definitive guide.

Manuel Smith (1981) *When I say 'No' I feel Guilty*, Bantam, New York.
One of the first books on assertiveness. First published in America in 1975.

Claude M. Steiner (1982) *Scripts People Live*, Bantam, New York.
Explains how the messages planted in our heads in childhood affect our
adult life and how to break their influence if you want to. Transactional
Analysis base.

Claire Walmesley (1991) *Assertiveness, the Right to be You*, BBC Publications, London.
Chirpy, practical introduction to assertiveness with workbook element.

Liz Willis and Jenny Daisley (1994) *Springboard Women's Development Workbook*, 3rd edition, Hawthorn Press, Stroud.
Practical workbook, in self-help format containing two substantial chapters on assertiveness. Widely used inside organizations. Written for women, but also relevant to men.

Sources of material for use on assertiveness courses

The following organizations provide a wide range of materials between them, from interactive video packages to simple booklets, and from photocopiable handouts to short videos.

The availability and price of individual products change so frequently that only an indication is given of the type of materials available at the time of writing. Contact the organizations direct for full details.

Ken and Kate Back Ltd, PO Box 33, Henley-on-Thames, Oxon RG9 1YN
Tel: 0491 411341 Fax: 0491 411094
A complete package including videos, overhead projector slides, notes, etc.

BBC Training Videos, Woodlands, 80 Wood Lane, London W12 0TT
Tel: 081 576 2016 Fax: 081 576 2867
A two-video package with trainers' notes and materials.

Connaught Training Ltd, Gower House, Croft Road, Aldershot, Hants GU11 3HR
Tel: 0252 331551
A video, activity manual and books.

The Domino Consultancy Ltd, 139 Ashley Road, Loughborough, Leics LE11 3AD
Tel: 0509 260270 Fax: 0509 260550
'Foundation' packs of materials for trainers and additional participant workbooks.

Dr Peter Honey, Ardingly House, 10 Linden Avenue, Maidenhead, Berks SL6 6HB
Tel: 0628 33946 Fax: 0628 33262
Series of questionnaires on Assertiveness Beliefs Check, Face to Face Assertiveness, and Telephone Assertiveness, all with commentary and interpretation guide, linked to Ken and Kate Back's work.

Longmans, Longman House, Burnt Mill, Harlow, Essex SM20 2JE
Tel: 0279 623927
An interactive video which either stands alone or is used as pre-course work.
Referred to by Colin Russell of British Telecom in his case study.

The National Extension College, 18 Brooklands Avenue, Cambridge CB2 2HN
Tel: 0223 316644
Trainers' manual and photocopiable materials.

Video Arts Ltd, Dumbarton Street, 68 Oxford Street, London W1N 9LA
Tel: 071 637 7288
Several videos with booklets and discussion guides.

Training assertiveness trainers

Many consultancies and training organizations offer training trainer events, either publicly or tailored for a specific organization. As there are several different approaches to assertiveness, when considering a training trainer event for assertiveness, find out carefully what their definition and philosophy is, what materials they use, how the course is run and by whom.

The following organizations are reputable, offer training assertiveness trainer courses, and have specialist skills. Contact them direct for further information.

Ken and Kate Back Ltd
PO Box 33, Henley-on-Thames, Oxon RG9 1YN
Tel: 0491 411341 Fax: 0491 411094

Workshops and materials suitable for a wide range of organizations. Enables in-company trainers to run a three-day assertiveness course, plus backup materials. The emphasis is on assertiveness at work.

Redwood Women's Training Association
20 North Street, Middleton, Manchester M24 6BD
Tel: 061 643 1986

Operates a highly respected national network of trainers who have been selected and trained in depth by Redwood. Successful trainers receive the Redwood Diploma and offer women-only, mixed-gender and men-only courses. Training trainer courses leading to the Diploma are offered regularly in several locations and are open to both self-employed and employed people.

The Springboard Consultancy
PO Box 69, Stroud, Glos GL5 5EE
Tel: 0453 878540 Fax: 0453 872363

Runs training assertiveness trainers' courses mostly in-house, tailored to the organization's requirements, but also 'public' courses for both in-house and freelance trainers. Also awards Springboard accreditation to women in-house and freelance trainers who are selected and trained to deliver The Springboard Women's Development Programme, which has a substantial assertiveness content.

Sample handouts

Assertive behaviour

> Assertiveness is a form of behaviour which demonstrates your self-respect and respect for others. This means that assertiveness is concerned with dealing with your own feelings about yourself and other people, as much as with the end result.

Being assertive means:

- being open and honest with yourself and other people
- listening to other points of view
- showing understanding of other people's situations
- expressing your ideas clearly, but not at the expense of others
- being able to reach workable solutions to difficulties
- making decisions, even if your decision is not to make a decision!
- being clear about your point of view
- dealing with conflict
- having self-respect and respect for other people
- being equal with others and retaining your uniqueness
- expressing feelings honestly and with care

Assertiveness is about respecting other people

Assertiveness is about building your own self-respect

Assertiveness is about dealing with your feelings

There are no set phrases, trick techniques, or magic words in assertiveness. There are five vital ingredients in any assertive process:

1 Listen
2 Demonstrate that you understand the other person
3 Say what you think or feel
4 Say specifically what you want to happen
5 Consider the consequences for yourself and others of any joint solutions

Passive and aggressive behaviour

Passive behaviour is:

- keeping quiet for fear of upsetting people
- avoiding conflict
- saying 'yes' when you want to say 'no'
- always putting other people's needs first
- not expressing your feelings
- going along with things you don't like or agree with
- apologizing excessively
- inwardly burning with anger and frustration
- being vague about your ideas and what you want
- justifying your actions to other people

- appearing indecisive

Aggressive behaviour is:

- getting your own way, no matter what
- getting your own point across at other people's expense
- getting people to do things they don't want to do
- being loud and violent
- being quiet and manipulative
- ignoring people
- putting people down, making them feel small
- using sarcasm
- interrupting others
- tricking people
- winning at all costs

Assertiveness scenarios

1 You are in the middle of a piece of work when you make a mistake. A colleague loses his/her temper and starts swearing at you and blaming you for other mistakes that have been made recently. You say to your colleague …

2 A colleague in another department has said that you will help them out, without consulting you first. You are extremely busy with your own work and furious that he/she should make such an assumption. You say to him/her …

3 You are having to embark on a new task, with some trepidation. Everyone is very busy and your boss has already explained the task to you very patiently. However, you now realize you didn't understand part of his/her explanation. You say to him her …

4 You are feeling taken for granted by your sister, who has asked you to fix things in her house several times in the last few weeks. She has just asked you yet again, and you really don't want to do it. You reply …

5 A colleague who has been having a bad time at work recently, sits down beside your desk, looking awful. You have an appointment in five minutes. You say …

6 Your partner returns home feeling very pleased, having paid the deposit on a holiday to Greece for you both, which was on 'special offer'. You had set your heart on going to America this year. You say to him/her …

Sample handout SITUATIONS IN WHICH TO BE MORE ASSERTIVE

Write down a list of ten situations in which you wish to become more assertive. Write beside each one how you deal with the situations now (passively, aggressively, manipulatively).

1

2

3

4

5

6

7

8

9

10

Now renumber on the right-hand side, making the one you would find easiest number 1 and the most difficult number 10.

Index

Further titles in the McGraw-Hill Training Series

THE BUSINESS OF TRAINING
Achieving Success in Changing World Markets
Trevor Bentley
ISBN 0-07-707328-2

EVALUATING TRAINING EFFECTIVENESS
Translating Theory into Practice
Peter Bramley
ISBN 0-07-707331-2

DEVELOPING EFFECTIVE TRAINING SKILLS
Tony Pont
ISBN 0-07-707383-5

MAKING MANAGEMENT DEVELOPMENT WORK
Achieving Success in the Nineties
Charles Margerison
ISBN 0-07-707382-7

MANAGING PERSONAL LEARNING AND CHANGE
A Trainer's Guide
Neil Clark
ISBN 0-07-707344-4

HOW TO DESIGN EFFECTIVE TEXT-BASED
OPEN LEARNING
A Modular Course
Nigel Harrison
ISBN 0-07-707355-X

HOW TO DESIGN EFFECTIVE COMPUTER-BASED
TRAINING:
A Modular Course
Nigel Harrison
ISBN 0-07-707354-1

HOW TO SUCCEED IN EMPLOYEE DEVELOPMENT
Moving from Vision to Results
Ed Moorby
ISBN 0-07-707459-9

USING VIDEO IN TRAINING AND EDUCATION
Ashly Pinnington
ISBN 0-07-707384-3

TRANSACTIONAL ANALYSIS FOR TRAINERS
Julie Hay
ISBN 0-07-707470-X

SELF-DEVELOPMENT
A Facilitator's Guide
Mike Pedler and
David Megginson
ISBN 0-07-707460-2

DEVELOPING WOMEN THROUGH TRAINING
A Practical Handbook
Liz Willis and
Jenny Daisley
ISBN 0-07-707566-8

DESIGNING AND ACHIEVING COMPETENCY
A Competency-Based Approach to Developing People and
Organizations
Editors: Rosemary Boam
and Paul Sparrow
ISBN 0-07-707572-2

TOTAL QUALITY TRAINING
The Quality Culture and Quality Trainer
Brian Thomas
ISBN 0-07-707472-6

CAREER DEVELOPMENT AND PLANNING
A Guide for Managers, Trainers and Personnel Staff
Malcolm Peel
ISBN 0-07-707554-4

SALES TRAINING
A Guide to Developing Effective Salespeople
Frank S. Salisbury
ISBN 0-07-707458-0

CLIENT-CENTRED CONSULTING
A Practical Guide for Internal Advisers and Trainers
Peter Cockman, Bill Evans
and Peter Reynolds
ISBN 0-07-707685-0

TRAINING TO MEET THE TECHNOLOGY CHALLENGE
Trevor Bentley
ISBN 0-07-707589-7

IMAGINATIVE EVENTS Volumes I & II
Ken Jones
ISBN 0-07-707679-6 Volume I
ISBN 0-07-707680-X Volume II
ISBN 0-07-707681-8 for set of Volume I & II